LIGHT WEIGHT CAMPING EQUIPMENT

Light Weight Camping Equipment

AND HOW TO MAKE IT

Gerry Cunningham
Margaret Hansson

CHARLES SCRIBNER'S SONS
NEW YORK

Copyright © 1976, 1959 Gerry Division, Outdoor
Sports Industries, Inc.

Library of Congress Cataloging in Publication Data

Cunningham, Gerry.
   Light weight camping equipment and how to make
it.

   Bibliography
   Includes index.
   1.   Camping—Outfits, supplies,
etc.   I.   Hansson, Meg, joint author.   II.   Title.
GV191.76.C86   1976   796.54′028   75-25855
ISBN 0-684-14262-7
ISBN 0-684-14261-9 (paper)

1 3 5 7 9 11 13 15 17 19 c/c 20 18 16 14 12 10 8 6 4 2
1 3 5 7 9 11 13 15 17 19 c/p 20 18 16 14 12 10 8 6 4 2

Printed in the United States of America

CONTENTS

LIST OF PLATES AND TABLES

LIST OF PROJECT INSTRUCTIONS

PREFACE

Family camping is one of the fastest growing leisure time activities in the country today. Often the destination is a public campsite, literally a tent city almost as crowded as the brick and asphalt one most people are escaping.

It surprises many people that the true wilderness areas, those served only by trails, are as accessible to them as the public campsites, and that they are rarely crowded. In days past, carrying your camp on your back meant heavy loads that only northwoods guides or the Army would tolerate. Today a family of five can spend several days alone in the backwoods carrying an average of less than 20 pounds apiece. Even a young couple can enjoy a camp away from the noise and smell of gasoline, if the father can manage 30 pounds and the mother can carry the baby in a kiddie carrier.

This book was conceived one evening when Meg Hansson was straining the budget to get six new sleeping bags in preparation for a Jackson Hole vacation, and Gerry Cunningham suggested she make them herself. Gerry is the founder and designer of the well known GERRY line of backpacking equipment, so he had much good advice to give. In its many editions this book has not only been used for the "do-it-yourself" projects it contains, but also as a source of information for evaluating and choosing good equipment.

Margaret Hansson
Gerry Cunningham

LIGHT WEIGHT CAMPING EQUIPMENT

CHAPTER I LEAVE NO TRACE

When did camping make the transition from occupation to recreation? For Daniel Boone and the pioneers it was definitely an occupation. For Tom Sawyer and Huck Finn it was recreation, an escape from Aunt Polly and the pressures of city life. The transition continues, and camping has become a form of recreation for millions of people the world over.

Unfortunately, although the change in outlook is well along, the techniques of camping often are still almost entirely those of the pioneer. The goal of the pioneer was to subdue nature, to put nature's resources to work for him. Whether or not he survived depended on his skill in shaping the environment to his own ends. A tree was seen as something to be cut down so he could plant crops in its place and construct something useful from its wood. A path was something to be widened and straightened and protected from the wear and tear of wagon wheels by a corduroy of logs. These were all logical means to an end. His job was to civilize the wilderness. The pioneer's methods have been so successful that the amount of land still wild has shrunk alarmingly.

Fortunately there are many people who are becoming aware that a place of solitude, a place of quiet, a place where man and his works are nowhere in evidence by sight, or sound, or smell, is a necessary haven to which they can escape from the daily pressures of modern life. A beautiful view in the distance is not enough. They want to immerse themselves in wilderness. They want to feel that they are the only humans to have set eyes on this particular vista. It is a renewal of the soul to believe themselves the exclusive beneficiary of the Creator for one short moment. If it could be calculated, the economic value of this recuperative power of the wilderness would probably be greater than the value of all the minerals and timber which the calculating commercial eye sees so well.

But appreciating the value of wilderness is not enough. If more and more people are going to seek the pleasures of solitude and quiet in wilderness, they are going to have to change from the Pioneer Camping Ethic to the Wilderness Camping Ethic, or they will destroy the very qualities they seek. In too many of the camping books found in bookstores today, the camping methods described are those of the pioneer. There are

3

elaborate fires and cooking centers to be built. Saws and axes and shovels are counted as necessary equipment. The construction of natural shelters, rustic furniture and various camp conveniences are counseled with the advice, "Why carry it with you when you can make it just like the pioneers did?" Bough beds, garbage pits, elaborate latrines are all part of the tradition.

And there is a modern technological offshoot that does as much thoughtless damage to the wilderness as do pioneer campcraft projects. Much advertised in the camping magazines are the new "disposables," without so much as an acknowledgment that there is a "disposal problem," commonly solved by throwing the used item in the nearest bush. We are offered disposable flashlights, sheets, pillow cases, tents, sleeping bags, fuel containers, cups, plates, silverware, cooking dishes, face tissues, food containers, towels, and cigarette lighters. Two of the more recent products that have found great favor among campers are aluminum foil for cooking and polyethylene sheeting for shelter and rain protection. Judging by the quantities of these two materials to be found around almost any campsite, they too are considered disposables.

As if this weren't enough, engineering and advertising have joined hands to produce still another wilderness destroyer. Conveniently forgetting what man learned back in Roman times, that the earth must be protected by pavement from the use of wheels, camping goods manufacturers offer us a great variety of motorized vehicles that boast an ability to claw their way into any wilderness area, saving man the effort of walking. Apparently there is some stigma connected with using your own muscles, because these vehicles are considered a manifestation of progress. Their riders might be called the Buck Rogers campers.

Last but not least, we have what might be called the gregarious campers. Their technique copies the Soviet enthusiasm for mass participation, or maybe they copy the popular trailer caravans that are organized to put as many people as possible in the same place at the same time. In any case, large groups do not belong in true wilderness. The organization of "trips" for 20 to 100 people is bound to leave its mark on the local ecology. The tolerances of different areas vary, but it is difficult to imagine how more than 10 people could spend a night in an undeveloped spot and leave no trace.

It is not only the mining, grazing, lumber, and tourist industries from which the wilderness must be protected. There are the camping techniques still being taught today from which it must also be protected. If our remaining wilderness areas are to support much greater traffic in the future than they are now subject to, we must abandon our pioneer methods and practice the Wilderness Camping Ethic to LEAVE NO TRACE.

The first requirement is a proper frame of mind. If, instead of offering awards of merit to see how closely a boy can emulate the pioneer, we change our goals to see if he can escape detection by leaving the least trace of his camp, the proper outlook will begin to develop. To start off on the right foot, here is a Wilderness Traveler's Creed:

I believe that man—the intelligent animal—can travel through the wilderness and LEAVE NO TRACE.

I will keep my group small.

I will keep my stay in one place short.

I will not cut down trees or branches.

I will not build fires, or if I do I will keep them small and scatter their remains when I leave.

I will leave no trash or other evidence of my stay in the wilderness.

I will LEAVE NO TRACE.

To accomplish this change of attitude, we will need the cooperation of all hunting and fishing clubs, sportsmen's clubs, scout leaders, camping teachers, outdoor writers, and anyone else who comes into contact with present and future wilderness users. The books in the bookstores and libraries must describe the techniques for camping without a trace. It won't be easy. To build a safe fire and completely eradicate it the next morning is often more difficult than to construct a large fire pit and cooking crane.

The Wilderness Camping Ethic does not mean that large camping groups can never be tolerated, but it must be recognized that large groups create wear and tear which must be confined to the use of maintained trails and campsites. It does not even preclude the use of motorized vehicles as long as their destructive qualities are recognized and confined to areas where ruts, erosion, and the destruction of small trees and meadowland is of little consequence. They should be used in areas where their noise and smell won't disturb wildlife and those who seek to escape from the ubiquitous gasoline engine. The Wilderness Camping Ethic definitely does not mean "locking up" the wilderness. Wilderness will best be preserved by exposing more people to its beauties, but we must do this in the least destructive way possible. The Wilderness Camping Ethic simply says that to preserve our remaining wilderness for everyone's enjoyment we must learn to travel through it and LEAVE NO TRACE.

The long range goal of the Wilderness Camping Ethic is to allow a much greater use of the wilderness without using it up, but the day-to-day rule of thumb can be more simply stated. To judge any act it is only necessary to ask yourself, "Will the next traveler, be he a couple of hours or a couple of years away, know that I have been here?" If this hypothetical "next traveler" will come to this spot and say, "Hmmm, someone has already been here," you have failed. As a matter-of-fact, even though you are using man-made facilities such as a road, trail, or campground, if all of us would operate on the personal conviction that no one should know that we personally have used this facility, the amount of traffic that can be borne by all facilities, natural or man-made, will be greatly increased without the expenditure of a single extra dollar.

Now, what means of travel are appropriate to the wilderness? Obviously, a powered vehicle with its noise, smell, and wheel treads is disqualified before it has gone 100 yards. How about a motor on a canoe? Once the wake has subsided it could be argued that no more trace has been left than if it had been paddled. However, the imprint of its sound is so far-reaching that one could say it leaves tremendous evidence of its whereabouts all the time. Oil slick on the waters would also be enough to betray its passage. A motor on a canoe cannot be said to leave no trace. We believe the same can be said of snowmobiles, which in addition to sound pollution while being used, often leave summertime evidence in the ground-off tops of small trees and bushes, and cause irreparable harm to once isolated wildlife.

Horses, as used today in long strings heavily laden and steel shod, require heavy trail maintenance. Overgrazing of high meadows has required the U.S. Forest Service to close many areas to horse packers. We hate to condemn the horse, because in intelligent hands he could qualify as a wilderness traveler who leaves no trace. Using the equipment and techniques of the backpacker, a couple of riders and their saddle horses could cover dozens of miles in a week of wilderness travel without leaving lasting signs. However, in the hands of most packers who make more money from large groups and elaborate camps, the horse is disqualified.

This leaves us foot travel and hand paddled canoe travel as the two acceptable means that leave no trace. In winter, skis or snowshoes qualify as foot travel.

There is the oft heard argument that "everyone isn't physically able to perform such strenuous exercise as walking and paddling." The claim is that these people have just as much right to enjoy our wilderness as the tough and rugged do. We take exception to that statement. We do not agree that if a person is physically out of shape he has as much right to enjoy the wilderness, any more than he has a right to enjoy any other sport for which he lacks the skill or conditioning.

There is more to enjoying the wilderness than just looking at it. Those who think they are experiencing wilderness by merely looking at the view can be accommodated by the many roads, boat rides, tramways, and helicopter trips available. It is for those who appreciate wilderness for its unique values of solitude, silence, and simplicity that we work to preserve it. We must not lose the last of our opportunities for solitude.

The person who considers himself unable to travel into the wilderness under his own power is probably the same one who plays golf from an electric golf cart to avoid the exercise. His longest walk is from the parking lot to the elevator in his office building. As long as progress is equated with not having to perform any physical exercise, there will be people who consider it unreasonable to walk or paddle. We do not believe these people have a right to destroy our wilderness.

Furthermore, anyone in this day and age who thinks that you have to be very tough and rugged to backpack, just isn't up-to-date. In areas where vehicles are prohibited, a 2- or 3-mile walk will get you away from most of the people, and those you may find at the end of the trail will have walked in and will be seeking the same peace and quiet that you are. Packs weighing only 18 pounds per person will give you everything you need for a comfortable, weatherproof camp. And these packs are easy on your back. Many people do it, from 6-year-old children to 60-year-old grandmothers.

It is true that the Boy Scout Handbook no longer carries instructions for making bough beds, but the same cannot be said for many other books on the market today. Judging from the condition of the trees and the litter of dead branches on the ground at most backpacking campsites, bough beds are still very much in vogue. Not enough boughs are used to give any real comfort. It just seems to be the appeal of the idea that calls forth the effort of construction.

Bough beds by far do the greatest damage, but the old craft of pioneer camping includes many other styles of bed that are calculated to leave plenty of trace. Digging hip holes, making log enclosures to contain the boughs or other padding, and constructing sapling frames set up on crotched sticks to hold rope or canvas bedsprings are all still advocated and described in detail. It is pointless. A comfortable summer temperature sleeping system requires no boughs and should weigh only 4½ to 5½ pounds. It is the keystone to a light weight backpacking outfit. If your sleeping bag is big and heavy, your whole outfit will suffer.

The sleeping bag will keep you snug and warm, but to avoid leaving the litter and destruction of a bough bed you must provide yourself with padding underneath. Urethane foam has been found to be the most practical material. A pad 1½″ to 2″ thick and just wide enough for the shoulders and long enough for the torso is satisfactory. It should be in a removable waterproof cover because it will be used around camp to sit on, cook on, lie on, and in many other ways. This pad is much more comfortable than any bed constructed in a campcraft class and will save the environment from wear and tear. We discuss sleeping systems in detail later on.

A good piece of equipment to hold sleeping bag and pad is a stuff sack about 32″ around and 20″ long. If properly packed, it will hold both the foam pad and the sleeping bag. The trick is to roll the pad up first and put it in, letting it expand around the outside of the sack. Make as large a hole as you can down the center of the pad. Then stuff one corner of the sleeping bag down to the bottom of the hole. Keep stuffing, and if you pack the bottom tight, you can cram the last bit into the top and still close the sack. This is how the modern wilderness traveler sleeps in comfort without using up any of the wilderness he is enjoying.

The construction of wilderness shelters is probably the most popular of all campcraft projects. These range all the way from lean-tos made from a single fir tree to a full log cabin with furniture. In the Colorado Rockies we have seen the remnants of the former with a 10″ log for the frame, and in the Sierra Nevada what appeared to have been a miniature log cabin that was made of 20 to 30 four-inch trees. Furthermore, instead of a thatch of its own boughs, it had been covered with orange polyethylene sheeting which had been left at the mercy of the wind when the campcrafter departed. Whoever he was, he left his big flapping orange mark for all to see.

What features should a shelter provide for the wilderness traveler? Protection from wet weather is the first thing that comes to mind. A less obvious but important protection is from insects, both the crawly kind and the flying kind. In fact it can be impossible to get a good night's sleep in some areas like Alaska and the Canadian Selkirks during mosquito season unless the mosquitoes can be kept out of your sleeping quarters. In the Adirondacks and the Maine woods during the blackfly season you may want a good insect-proof tent just to eat your lunch in. Rustic shelters give no protection from insects. The last important protection a good shelter can give, which is most appreciated in cold damp weather, is as a place to get in out of the wind. The temperature inside a good tent can be 10°F higher than the outside air temperature. Most campcraft shelters are pretty open to the breezes.

A modern tent that requires no cutting or digging comes complete with separate rainfly, guy lines, aluminum poles, and pegs and can weigh less than 2½ pounds per person. A single layer tent that pitches by stringing between trees can weigh less than 1 pound per person and still have nylon netting to protect against insects. The advantage of the heavier tent with the separate rainfly is that it solves the condensation problem. Pitched in a sensible, well-drained spot, a tent with a waterproof sewn-in floor eliminates any need to dig up the ground cover in the well-known "ditching the tent" ritual. Tents are discussed in detail later.

There is no need to cut poles and pegs at your campsite. Some tents can be pitched by stringing them between trees. This requires a little searching for a suitable spot, and about 40 feet of nylon cord. The next lightest method of pitching is a single aluminum pole at each end. A stronger and more roomy method is to use two poles running through sleeves sewn to the sidewalls of the tent. Tent pegs made of thin aluminum rod will hold in all firm sods. Loose duff and gravel requires a fold of aluminum or a plastic peg with a little more bearing area. Granted you can save a few ounces if you don't carry poles and pegs, but you will most certainly advertise your use of the spot. At only 2½ pounds per person, why not be a modern wilderness traveler and use a backpacker's tent that leaves no trace?

The most obvious difference between man and the animals that live in the wilderness is that animals do not use fire. The remains of man's fires have been used to trace his wanderings far back into pre-history. The problem is obvious. Man's longest lasting refuse, charcoal, is also the one which he alone brings into the wilderness, and he seems to be quite proud of it. Look around any spot that has been used as a campsite before, and you will usually find half a dozen fireplaces. We seem to have a nesting instinct that requires us to make our own personal hearth before we feel at home in a place. Here again, the campcraft books are at fault. Pages and pages are devoted to instructions for building trench fires, keyhole fires, tepee fires, crisscross fires, and many more. A fire-building tradition is being taught, but the techniques of eradicating all traces of the fire before the camper leaves is almost never discussed in these books.

Because modern dehydrated backpacking foods have all but eliminated complicated cooking chores, the problem of a fire that leaves no trace is not as difficult as it used to be. There are two ways to approach the problem. One is to carry a stove. There are a few good stoves on the market for backpackers. When stoves are properly used, less than 8 ounces of fuel will cook 2 meals per day for 3 people on a weekend hike. The stove itself weighs only 7 ounces. The keys to the efficiency are in using a deep well cooker that concentrates the heat around the bottom and sides of the pot, and in doing the cooking inside the tent, out of the wind. The pot requires a lid to keep the heat and moisture inside, and to make the artificial fire practical it is necessary to conserve the heat so that it goes into the pot and is not wafted away by the breezes. If you use a stove you must carry all of your refuse and garbage out with you.

However, we must face the fact that the smell and warmth of a wood fire are two of the simple joys of camping. We compromise and carry both a stove and a fire grill on most trips. We use the stove when it rains, or when a wood fire would be unsafe, or when an area has already been devastated by too much wood gathering and fire building. When we can, we build a wood fire. Obviously, if you use a stove it is easy to leave no trace, but to eradicate the signs of a wood fire requires skill. First the fire must be safely built. If the area has been heavily used, there will be old fireplaces. Select the most satisfactory one and use it. If you are in virgin country, bear in mind that the floor of most evergreen forests is made of a very burnable duff composed of the fallen needles from the trees. In other forests, the leaves decay into a burnable covering, so fires built directly on the forest floor are absolutely forbidden under any circumstances. A patch of mineral dirt or bare rock must be found, with no exposed tree roots. Fire can burn along a tree root for days and eventually ignite the tree many feet from the original site. It isn't difficult to find dirt or gravel around streams or lakes. If the forest floor is thin, it may be temporarily removed to expose the mineral dirt underneath and replaced when you leave. It is also possible to build up a thick layer of gravel on top of the duff, but this presents problems when it is time to get rid of it. Green grass sod makes a good fire base but the fire destroys the grass unless you lay a base of stones to protect the grass from the heat. Every locality presents a different problem. Basically it is essential to: (a) recognize burnable ground cover like pine duff, dry grass, and dead leaves, and (b) keep this material away from your fire so heat or sparks can't start it smoldering.

A fire that leaves no trace must be kept small. This also makes it easy to gather the wood without leaving a trace. Any wood you can break in your hands or against a rock will be suitable for a small fire. Saws, axes, hatchets, and large knives are useless weight to the modern wilderness traveler. A dozen thumb-size sticks about a foot long are sufficient for cooking a meal or two, and you gather only enough to do the job. If wood is so convenient that a huge pile can be accumulated, it will be easy enough to collect a little more if you run out, so leave it where it is. If it is scarce, instead of being gathered into piles of surplus, left to rot on the ground, it is best left where it is. Gather only enough to use.

It is easy to build a ring of stones to contain your small fire and support a simple grill for your pots. No elaborate fireplaces are needed. If wind is a problem, fit the stones closer, and build a little higher on the windward side. Flat rocks are the easiest to build with, but in any case you should be able to carry them in one hand or they will be too large for a fireplace that will leave no trace.

Now you have cooked your dinner, had a good sleep, cooked breakfast, and burned all of your burnable garbage and trash. You have washed your dishes back away from the stream, using soap, or a biodegradable detergent. You are ready to hit the trail again and leave no trace of last night's camp. If you have been a good wilderness traveler so far, this won't be hard. One thing that you might not think of is that charcoal is pure carbon and will last forever, no matter what you do with it. Wood ashes on the other hand will dissolve into the ground with the next rain. During the last few minutes of your fire, don't add any wood, but keep scraping all the embers close together so they burn themselves to ash. To put the fire out, pour water on it while you stir it up with a stick until it, and the ground underneath and between the rocks, is thoroughly wet.

Now, here is another thing you might not think of. A lot of the food packing material you threw in the fire looked like paper, but in fact had aluminum foil inside. Rake through your wet ashes and pick out all of the aluminum foil and anything else that didn't burn. Wad this up for your trash bag and carry it out with you. After all, you carried it in.

If there is any unused firewood left, scatter it around naturally. If anyone else selects that same spot, the wood will be there for them to pick up, but a neat little pile won't advertise the fact that they weren't the first to discover this particular corner of the wilderness. The stones from the fireplace should be replaced in their original locations, or if there are lots of stones around on the ground you can scatter them inconspicuously. Each location has its particular problems. It is up to your skill and ingenuity to leave no trace. Next, the ashes and remaining charcoal must be gotten rid of. Since they are soaking wet, this can be a mess. We usually save two of the plastic bags from our food packaging to use as gloves. Neither ashes nor charcoal is indigenous to your campsite. About the only thing you can do is to scatter them in the least conspicuous place possible. If you have followed these suggestions skillfully, the ashes will be dead and wet, but this is the time to make certain. You don't want to be scattering any live coals about. If anything is too warm to pick up in your bare hands, it should be considered dangerous and wetted down and stirred up again. Large chunks of charcoal are suspect, as are large sticks that didn't burn up.

With stones and ashes scattered, only the fire base remains. Gravel and rocks can be put back where they came from. If a thin layer of forest floor was removed, it should be replaced now. Then the whole area can be smoothed over with your feet or a dead branch, to blend it into its surroundings. Time and nature will do the rest.

Sound like a lot of work? Well, it isn't as much work as building a bonfire and a large fireplace, and keeping it supplied with firewood. A little practice and you do it all without thinking, until you run across a beautiful spot to camp that presents a unique challenge to your skill. Under those conditions we have gone to considerable trouble to leave no trace, but we have always felt that it was worth the effort.

There is one more subject that should be touched on, considering the American preoccupation with the disposal of human wastes. Any camping magazine will alert you to the fact that there are more brands and styles of toilets for wheeled campers than any other accessory. When you concentrate high use within a limited area, waste disposal is indeed one of the things you must provide facilities for. However, wilderness camping tends to spread the use and makes waste disposal less of a problem. This is one situation in which the animals leave more of a trace than humans like to. But of all the things man leaves strewn about in the wilderness, his droppings are the most readily biodegradable and will return to nature the quickest. The U.S. Forest Service has come up with the following recommendations for wilderness waste disposal:

1. Select a suitable spot at least 50 feet from any open water.
2. Dig a hole 8″ to 10″ in diameter and *no more than* 6″ to 8″ deep, to stay within the "biological disposer" layer of soil. Save the sod or dirt.
3. After use, fill the hole with loose soil and tramp the sod back in place.
4. Nature will do the rest in a few days.

You see, for a skillful wilderness traveler it is entirely possible to enjoy the wilderness without consuming it or destroying it. If only skilled wilderness travelers were allowed to use the wilderness, it could bear much greater traffic than it is now subject to. But, we do not yet have a lot of skillful wilderness travelers, and much damage has already been done. Can we not start at once to reverse the trend?

We would like to suggest that all of you do two things when you go out into the back country. First, clean up the signs left by others before you. Ordinary litter is easy. Just carry a plastic litter bag in your pack and pick the litter up along the trail and around the campsite. A few years ago this would have been a futile project, but now the trails are cleaner and our families rarely pick up more than a pound of litter on a weekend trip. The lift you can give to a much used campsite is usually considerable. A lot of the litter will be burnable. There are often the remnants of campcraft projects like bough beds, cooking cranes, tent poles, and pegs. In most cases these can be used as firewood before any fresh firewood is gathered. If yours is one of those sites that has a dozen big and little fireplaces, you can obliterate the infrequently used ones, and give these spots a chance to go back to nature. Subsequent wilderness travelers will use the one that is left. The last thing you can do is to go through the ashes in the fireplace for unburnables and carry them out in your litter bag. Granted, you can't make a large, heavily used campsite disappear without a trace, but you can clean it up so the traces of man's use are kept to a minimum.

The second suggestion is more subtle. On your way out, stop everyone you meet on the way in and, with your litter bag in hand, ask them if they have any trash you can carry out for them. Many will appreciate this consideration, but the greatest impact will be on those to whom it never occurred that trash was to be carried out and not thrown on the ground. They may have nothing to give you right then, but your hint may come to mind the next time they start to toss away a candy wrapper.

The time has come to change our camping ways from those of the Pioneer to those of the Wilderness Traveler—and LEAVE NO TRACE.

CHAPTER II MATERIALS FOR
LIGHT WEIGHT EQUIPMENT

Extensive field trials, experimentation, and testing have proved that of the many products available on the market only a few are adaptable to the high specifications demanded by light weight climbing and hiking gear. This chapter on materials is an attempt to give the reader the information and data he will need to make an intelligent choice among the hundreds of materials available. We will include all the items that go into making the light weight equipment described in this book, such as fabrics, webbing, hardware, leather, and fillers for sleeping bags and clothing. The information will be useful not only for construction of personal equipment, but also as a guide to purchasing durable and suitable equipment.

Community and mail order sources of materials and services will be listed. Most of the sources which carry materials of a specialized nature will send catalogs and samples upon request. Samples may then be compared for the required performance characteristics. There is no more disheartening fate than to spend hours making a piece of equipment in which the workmanship is of top quality, only to find that it is worthless after a season's use because of poor or improper materials.

FABRICS

Most items of camping equipment involve the use of fabric in one way or another. One of the interesting facets of designing and making one's own equipment is the adaptation of new fabrics and materials to their most efficient use. New fabrics may include any of the myriad synthetics, blends of synthetics and natural fibers, or they may be entirely new developments in fabrics made from natural fibers. Science is always a jump ahead of the consumer. Miraculous though they are said to be, each fabric made of a new fiber must be thoroughly tested to see what it will do, publicity notwithstanding. A new fabric may be truly miraculous for one purpose, but totally unsuitable for others. In other cases advertisers get carried away and performance falls far short of promise. Fabrics must be tested for the specific job they are to do.

CONSTRUCTION

The fabric construction with which we are most familiar is the plain weave. A plain woven fabric is woven with one fill yarn alternating over and under one warp yarn. The tightest fabrics are woven in this manner. Good examples of such a weave are broadcloth and muslin.

Due to the sharp angle the yarns take in a plain tight weave, the tear strength is relatively low. Generally speaking, the sleazier the fabric, or less tight the weave, the higher the tear strength because several yarns take up the strain at once. Parachute fabric, for instance, is very sleazy but wonderfully adapted to the absorption of the shock of an opening parachute due to its very high tear strength. Fabrics of a specific construction are designed and suited to specific jobs.

There are variations of plain weaves too. Oxford cloth, as an example, is a plain woven fabric where two parallel yarns are woven as one. Flat duck is woven with two warp yarns as one, giving high abrasion resistance. In poplin extra heavy threads run in one direction producing a ribbed effect. All are variations of plain weaves.

In order to increase the abrasion resistance of a fabric it will sometimes be woven with one thread passing over two or three yarns to avoid the sharp angle bends of the plain weave. This method of weaving results in a fabric with a diagonal ribbed surface. Some examples of this weave are twill, whipcord, denim, drill, and sateen. Sateen is an extreme case—a warp yarn will sometimes cross as many as seven fill yarns. A smooth lustrous surface results, but with such long exposed floaters, poor abrasion resistance results.

Mosquito netting is still another construction. It can be any loosely woven netting fabric but for camping equipment it should be of marquisette construction rather than bobbinet. In marquisette the warp yarns are twisted between each filling yarn (called a leno weave) to keep them from slipping and pulling apart as will happen, for instance, with cheesecloth. Bobbinet is a weave similar to chicken wire. This hexagonal weave allows it to stretch and pull out of shape very easily, making it unsuitable for camping equipment. All mosquito netting should be of nylon since it is much stronger for this basically fragile construction. There are also heavier mesh fabrics which make good back support panels for pack boards because their large holes allow free circulation of air.

An entirely different problem is presented when the fabric consists of something besides woven yarns, as in coated or waterproof fabrics. Any type of plastic or rubber coated fabric should be constructed with a specially woven base fabric. The coating itself lowers the tear strength of the fabric by localizing the strain of the tear to a very few threads, or even a single thread. The base fabric must allow for this and be constructed with a basket weave, many parallel threads crossing loosely. This makes for a smooth flat surface for adhesion of the coating and will allow the strain of a tear to be taken by many threads at once resulting in a much stronger fabric. Such a heavy duty coated fabric is U.S. Rubber's Fiberthin or Reeves-Vulcan Coverlite. The light weight coated fabrics usually have a twill or plain weave base.

This general description of construction of fabrics will give some idea as to the choice of a fabric for a specific purpose. First decide on the job to be performed and then choose a fabric that will do it.

PROPERTIES

Weight Weight as a property of a fabric is self-evident. The lighter the fabric, the lighter the finished product. However, weight is also a general indication of the tear strength and abrasion resistance. The heavier the fabric, the greater the tear strength and abrasion resistance for the same fiber.

The weights given for fabrics are usually stated by the weaver as ounces per square yard (of the fabric) and due to variations in the weaving process can vary as much as ten per cent in either direction. In coated fabrics variation may be even greater due to irregularity in the thickness of the coating. Some fabrics go by weight per running yard (usually the very narrow ones and the very wide ones) so it is important that the basis for the weight be stated and converted to ounces per square yard.

Porosity Porosity is the ability of a fabric to allow the passage of air. This is usually stated as cubic feet of air passed per minute, for each square foot of fabric area, at a wind pressure equal to 32 miles per hour ($\frac{1}{2}$" hydrostatic pressure).

There are two rough methods for home comparison of porosity. Place a piece of fabric over your mouth and blow through it, holding the fabric tightly against the lips. Quickly blow through another sample fabric. The difference in porosity, if great enough, can be sensed. Another check is to hold the fabric to a strong light and note the amount of light passage. Care must be taken with this method though for, in twill weaves especially, maximum light passage is seen when the fabric is tilted off the vertical. Tilt the fabric at various angles to see the maximum light. The more light passage, the more porous the fabric. Porosity is important as an indication of a fabric's wind resistance.

Tear Strength Tear strength, as opposed to tensile strength, is of great practical importance for it is here that failure will occur in the field. Tear strength is a function of both the weave and the fiber used. For example, it is important to know how much force is required to tear a tent which might become snagged on a tree branch, or perhaps the tear strength of a pair of pants caught on a sharp projection of rock. At least it will be useful to know the comparative performance of various fabrics under these conditions.

Tensile strength, on the other hand, is related to a bursting of the fabric, depending more on the fiber used, and is of much less practical importance.

Fabrics should have a balanced construction so that tear strength is approximately equal in both directions along the warp and fill. This is difficult to do with mixed fibers, as in fabrics with cotton warp and nylon fill.

To measure the tear strength of a fabric, cut a slit in the direction of the weave and punch a hole in one of the two legs formed. Hook in the hole of the leg a spring scale reading up to ten pounds or so and pull the other leg until the fabric tears, noting how much force is required to *continue* the tear. Comparative tests are possible without the scales if necessary. Be sure the tear is always started with a cut, and the force required to continue the tear is observed.

Abrasion Resistance Abrasion resistance is obviously one of the most important properties of fabrics for such items of equipment as pants and packs, but one for which it is almost impossible to establish valid tests. Such things as abrasive surface, pressure of contact, tension in the fabrics, determination of point of failure, are all variables that have a great influence on the outcome of any test. These variables are very hard to control precisely and to date there is no method known that correlates with actual wear in service. No effort has been made here to evaluate abrasion resistance. Suffice it to say that the fabrics recommended here seem to be performing well in service.

Water Repellency Water repellents are extremely variable in their performance. No completely satisfactory test has been developed to rate their qualities.

A simple comparison test can be made on a number of samples, however. Stretch samples of fabric tightly over the top of a bowl. Pour a constant quantity of water into the center of the sample from a constant height. About one quart of water poured slowly from a height of one foot will give results. Any great difference in the water repellency of various samples will be shown by the quantity of water allowed to pass through into the bowl. It is best to run several samples of each fabric for more accurate results.

Some water repellents are much more durable than others and it is advisable to repeat the test after hanging the samples out to weather for two or three weeks. More will be said of repellents for home use later.

Color   It would at first seem that color is entirely a matter of personal choice. However, there are two points to be considered before allowing aesthetic feelings to take over. First, very dark colors are excellent absorbers of the sun's heat. For summer cool stick to light and medium colors. For winter warmth use dark colors. Secondly, if visibility is important remember that bright orange has the highest visibility against snow or in fog and bright yellow is more visible in most other circumstances. If these conditions don't have to be met then any whim can be satisfied with any color at all. If red is desired in a cotton fabric, be sure it is vat dyed as other dyes in bright red are apt to rub off on white shirts, etc. The browns and greens blend with nature and leave less trace.

FIBERS

There are many things that could be said about fibers in this day of man-made synthetics. The search for the perfect fiber goes on. It occupies the time of hundreds of scientists. These men can predict the properties of a fiber of a given molecular structure; they can build a fiber, and thus a fabric, almost to order. But it seems there is always a drawback for each set of advantages. Designers must use the fiber with the best combination of advantages and either overcome its drawbacks or live with them.

Experience and testing by many climbers and campers have proved many of the old standbys very suitable. The performance of many of the newer fibers and fabrics is not so well known. The following descriptions of fibers will cover those that have proved to be the best suited for construction of light weight gear.

Nylon   Nylon is still the strongest fabric for its weight in general use. In spite of disadvantages it outranks all other common fibers where toughness and light weight are desirable.

Nylon is usually woven as a continuous filament yarn. Its filament is a tough solid elastic rod drawn out to a fine diameter suitable for weaving. It is this construction which gives nylon fabric both its advantages and disadvantages.

Its disadvantages are of two kinds—those which can be overcome through proper use of the fiber and fabric, and those which have to be put up with. Those disadvantages which can be overcome by suitable techniques are:

1. Nylon's slipperiness makes a sleazy fabric unless it is carefully woven and heat set in the finishing operation. This slippery quality also causes the cut edges of the fabric to fray very badly unless finished seams are used or the edges are melted to fuse the yarns together.
2. Nylon, being a hard round fiber, requires the use of proper techniques and close controls in order to be woven into a tight fabric. It does not "pack" easily in weaving.
3. Nylon thread is difficult to use in home sewing machines due to its elasticity. With practice and minimum tension adjustment, nylon becomes easier to use and this very elasticity makes it ideal for locations of stress.

Those important disadvantages which have to be put up with are:

1. Nylon is not a wet weather fabric. No matter how tightly it is woven, the solid round rod characteristic of its fibers prevents it from retaining any water repellent treatment for very long, especially after a few weeks' weathering. Nylon clothing tends to soak through sooner than a good repellent treated cotton in a steady rain.
2. Condensation problems are more acute in nylon tents and clothing than in cotton. Some authorities say that nylon is less permeable to water vapor than cotton, but recent textile research tends to refute this. Because nylon has a higher conductivity than cotton it gets colder, and this encourages condensation. The fact remains that the condensation of moisture inside a nylon tent or one with a nylon lining is more disagreeable than with cotton fabrics. Some preliminary work done by Gerry indicates there is actually less moisture pickup by weight with nylon, but what there is is present on the surface of the fabric, making it "feel" much wetter. If the nylon is shaken, it drops more of its moisture than cotton. In spite of this the most successful high altitude tents are nylon (with cotton liners).

There is another important type of nylon fabric, usually a heavier balanced weave pack fabric. In this type the filaments are shorter and finer and spun into a fiber much the way cotton and wool are. The resulting woven fabric has a natural fiber feel, great strength, and greater ability to retain water repellent treatment. One such type of nylon fabric is Cordura.

Even with these disadvantages nylon's toughness, elasticity, and light weight will make it the choice where lightest weight is required. There are times when another fabric must be chosen such as when high humidity and rain dictate the use of cotton, but where you want a parka and a pair of wind pants that will fit into the hip pockets, a light nylon is the thing.

Kerlar This is a new low-stretch fabric used for sailboat sails. Although it is stronger than nylon, its advantages for backpacking gear remain to be exploited.

Cotton Old reliable cotton still has important advantages. Pima or Egyptian cottons have extra long fibers and make superior fabrics. Pima cotton is an American Egyptian cotton grown in the Southwest from Egyptian seed. It must have at least a 1⅜" fiber length.
Some of the important advantages of cotton are:

1. Less disagreeable condensation.
2. Cotton will accept and hold any water repellent treatment.
3. Cotton can be packed easily into a tightly woven, wind resistant fabric.

Its disadvantages are:

1. It has a low tear strength.
2. It is subject to mildew and rot.

Cotton is often used in conjunction with nylon in order to retain the advantages of both. Pima-nylon fabrics are such a combination. These, however, range in quality from the English Wyncol fabric (Everest fabric) of extremely low porosity, to cheap fabrics of very high porosity whose only similarity to Wyncol fabric is their use of both nylon and cotton yarns.

Wool Wool is used to advantage chiefly in shirts, socks, mittens, and pants. It retains its springiness and hence its warmth when wet, though the strength is lowered appreciably. Where abrasion resistance is important such as in climbing pants, wool is not as suitable as some of the synthetics.
The use of wool as a sleeping bag filler will be discussed later.

Dacron Dacron is a synthetic almost as strong as nylon though it lacks nylon's elasticity. The lack of elasticity in dacron gives it an advantage over nylon when it is used as sewing thread. Continuous filament dacron sewing thread is much easier to handle in home sewing machines than nylon. The lack of elasticity also makes it possible to weave very firm tight fabrics from Dacron.

It is also slightly more resistant to weather and sun than nylon. For these reasons it is used for the best boat sails. However, sail fabrics are so closely woven as to approximate the performance of a coated fabric.

Dacron's use as a sleeping bag filler will be discussed later.

Orlon All of the natural and most of the synthetic fibers, including nylon and Dacron, deteriorate upon exposure to direct sunlight. Orlon has been developed specifically to resist this deterioration. Generally, except for tents which are left up all summer year after year, this advantage is not of too great importance.

Orlon, in its spun state, where it is cut into short lengths and spun into yarn as natural fibers are, closely resembles wool. It is considerably stronger than wool especially when wet, and makes excellent clothing.

FABRIC COATINGS

Putting an actual plastic coating on a fabric is the only way to waterproof it completely. This also means that the fabric is completely impermeable to water vapor. This in turn means that vapor will be trapped inside, and such a coated fabric must be used only where ventilation is adequate. The so-called "breathable" coatings are a compromise but condensation will be a problem under some conditions and they leak under heavy rains. There are multi-layered coatings of urethane on the market which breathe, but more importantly have considerable thickness and insulating value. This is the real reason they don't condense. Condensation will take place any time warm moist air is in contact with cold air or a cold surface. Ventilation helps to keep the moisture content down, but "breathable" fabrics can pass only a minute quantity of vapor compared with what can be ventilated out. Fabrics that are thick enough to provide some insulation, on the other hand, give the inside surface a chance to warm up above the dew point. This, more than the breathability, produces the "no sweat" comfort in clothing and tents.

Table of Comparative Textile
Fiber Properties

FIBER	Nylon	Dacron	Orlon	Cotton	Wool
Tensile strength in gms/denier	6.8	6.1	4.5	3.9	1.4
Elongation before breaking	22%	12%	16%	5%	30%
Effect of heat	melts at 482°F	melts at 480°F	sticky at 455°F	scorches at 500°F	scorches at 400°F
Effect of sunlight and weathering	loses strength	loses less strength	very resistant	loses strength	loses strength

Table of Comparative Textile
Fiber Properties (cont.)

FIBER	Nylon	Dacron	Orlon	Cotton	Wool
Resistance to moths	wholly	wholly	wholly	wholly	none
Resistance to mildew	wholly	wholly	finish may be attacked	very poor	good

There are many fabrics coated with a large variety of compounds. Few of these compounds are suitable for camping equipment. Most are very heavy imitation leather fabrics, or those used for heavy protective tarpaulins. Some stiffen and crack after weathering, some stiffen and crack at low temperatures. Some compounds are easily peeled from the base fabric, some have little abrasion resistance. Most of them reduce the tear strength of the fabric, as mentioned before. Some of the most suitable compounds for climbing and camping gear which take hard wear are polyvinyl butyral, the low temperature vinyl compounds, neoprene, and polyurethane. A long weathering test of about two or three months will usually tell the story. A scratch with the fingernail or rubbing the coated surfaces together will then indicate any deterioration in the coating.

A two-side coated or impregnated fabric will weigh about half again as much as a single coated fabric, but has the advantage that a leak will not develop if the coating on one side wears through. Also, with the double coatings interconnecting through the fabric, the adhesion to the base fabric is much better.

A good many of the best fabrics mentioned in this book are so specialized that they are obtainable only from dealers using this kind of fabric. These sources are listed at the end of this chapter. However, in many cases local yardgoods stores and awning shops carry very suitable fabrics.

Table of Comparative Fabric Properties

Fabric Description	Weight Per Square Yard	Air Porosity (cu.ft./sq.ft./min @ $\frac{1}{2}''$ H_2O pressure)	Tongue Tear Strength (average lbs.)
HEAVY PACK FABRICS			
Double filled army duck, cotton	12.1 oz.		17
Army nylon duck (unwaterproof)	6.5 oz.		50
Nylon oxford			
Nylon spun filament			

Table of Comparative Fabric Properties (cont.)

Fabric Description	Weight Per Square Yard	Air Porosity (cu.ft./sq.ft./min @ ½" H₂O pressure)	Tongue Tear Strength (average lbs.)
HEAVY CLOTHING FABRICS			
11 oz. cotton denim	11 oz.		12.5
Army 9 oz. sateen	9 oz.		14.4
Orlon whipcord	8.5 oz.		8.0
Wool kersey	9 oz.		3.5
WIND RESISTANT CLOTHING AND TENT FABRICS			
Nylon pima oxford (army specs.)	5 oz.	3.0	9.5
LIGHT WEIGHT CLOTHING AND TENT FABRICS			
Rip-stop nylon (untreated)	1.9 oz.	10.7	6.1
Rip-stop nylon (silicone doped)	2 oz.	1.05	7.0
Army 120 x 120 cotton balloon cloth	2.25 oz.	89.0	1.5
English Egyptian cotton	2.75 oz.	4.11	2.9
Nylon taffeta	2.1 oz.	2.53	6.6
COATED FABRICS			
Horcolite (polyvinyl butyral)	2.75 oz.		5
Coverlite (neoprene)	6.5 oz.		7
Fiberthin (vinyl)	5 oz.		9
Nylsurf (polyurethane)	2.6 oz.		3
K-kote (polyurethane)			
MISCELLANEOUS FABRICS			
Nylon mosquito netting (army specs)	1.6 oz.		3
Nylon shoe mesh	9 oz.		35

NARROW FABRICS

The term narrow fabrics as it is used here applies to all kinds of webbing, tapes, cords, laces, and thread. The discussion will be limited to those products which are adapted to climbing and camping gear.

WEBBING

Webbing is a stout firmly woven narrow fabric. Strap grade webbing (the only grade useful here) comes in various widths—⅝", ¾", 1½", 2", etc. The narrower widths, ⅝" to ¾", are the widths suitable for the various parts of pack harness that don't bear against the body with the full weight of the pack, such as attachment straps, and the lower sections of shoulder straps. This width is also for peg loops in tents.

The wider widths, $1\frac{1}{2}''$ to $2''$ webbing, are suitable for pack shoulder straps and other portions of pack harness that bear the weight of the pack on the body. The wider width is used for the obvious reason that narrow straps cut the shoulders and become extremely uncomfortable. The webbing for these straps should be very firm, not limp.

In the fabrication of most packs cotton webbing is satisfactory since it is firm, tough, and close-woven. Nylon webbing has the advantage of being rot and mildew proof, but its greater strength is not needed here. Only nylon webbing is suitable for tent loops due to its toughness and abrasion resistance. Great strain is placed on these loops and any but nylon may be cut by rocks and stakes.

Cargo parachute shroud lines are often made of $\frac{1}{2}''$ or $1''$ tubular nylon webbing. Army surplus stores frequently carry this webbing and it is very suitable for many of the pack and tent applications described. Since this webbing is tubular, when it is used with buckles and as pack straps it should be stitched together flat lengthwise once or twice. The ends of all nylon webbing should be melted in a flame to prevent fraying. The end of the webbing is held close to the flame until it begins to melt.

TAPE

Tape is by definition a narrow fabric of light weight. As referred to here it is woven with *two* finished edges. Bias or self fabric tapes are not suitable. Some nylon tapes have melted edges but they will fray eventually.

Tapes of $\frac{1}{2}''$ or $\frac{3}{4}''$ width are most frequently used for reinforcing along lines of stress in tents and packs and as draw and tie tapes in tents, sleeping bags, and other gear. The $\frac{3}{4}''$ to $1''$ widths are useful in the binding of seams to prevent cut edges of the fabric from fraying.

Twill tape is a standard sewing item stocked in most notions departments. Even stronger and giving a better finished appearance is a *good quality* grosgrain ribbon.

CORD

Nylon parachute shroud line (cord) with a diameter of $\frac{7}{32}''$ and a tensile strength of 550 pounds serves excellently for many purposes: pack drawstrings, packboard lashing, tent guylines. Several accessories such as drawstring clamps and guyline tighteners are made specially to fit this cord. The best parachute shroud line is constructed with an outside nylon sheath braided around several central nylon core yarns. The plaited type without the finely woven sheath tends to snag on rocks and branches. All cut ends of shroud lines should be melted in a flame to prevent fraying. Army surplus stores stock this cord regularly.

LACE

Shoe lace material, nylon and cotton, by the yard makes excellent light drawstrings for clothing, ditty bags, cases, and such. It makes fine tieback tapes to hold mosquito netting and tent doors out of the way. It is also used as reinforcing along lines of stress in tents. Nylon lace does not stay tied very well unless it is the fuzzy spun nylon variety.

THREAD

Thread is extremely important to all items of equipment since the seams, except in the lightest fabrics, are generally the weakest points. Cotton thread is not strong enough for most uses in climbing and camping equipment and will not be discussed. If it must be used, go to a tailor's or upholstery shop and get a good strong mercerized grade without knots or slubs.

Of the strong synthetic threads Dacron is the easiest to use in the home sewing machine because it does not stretch and drop stitches, as we have said before. Nylon, however, still has the edge where strength really counts. Usually, the heavier threads are easier to handle, size E being about as large as any home sewing machine can take. The smaller sizes, A and B, are generally available at notions counters. Shoe repair shops sometimes use the larger sizes. Dual duty threads are strong and useful. This thread has a Dacron core and cotton wrap. Tensions are easier to handle than nylon because there is less stretch.

For very heavy sewing, such as attaching shoulder straps to heavy pack fabric, it is best to sew by hand using a large needle or stitching awl. For this kind of stitching one of the center core threads from nylon parachute shroud lines or nylon fish line make the strongest possible stitch.

Table of Comparative Thread
Strengths in Pounds

COTTON—6 cord

size	40	36	30	24	20	16	Coats & Clark Button & Carpet	Waxed Stitching Awl Thread
strength soft	2.3	2.6	3	3.5	4	4.6		
strength mercerized	2.7	2.9	3.5	4.4	5.1	6.4	8.5	20

SYNTHETICS

size				B	C	D	E	F
nylon strength				4.5	6	7.5	9	13.5
Dacron strength				4	5.4	6.7	8.1	12
dual duty					60/36	36/16		
Dacron core/cotton wrap					3	6		

INSULATION

All of the materials used for filling sleeping bags, sleeping bag pads, and insulating garments will be considered as insulation. *Any* material which will sufficiently deaden the air against circulation, be it *eiderdown* or *steelwool,* will provide the same degree of insulation per unit of thickness. This is not a commonly known fact but its application to insulated camping gear is apparent. The conduction of heat through the insulating material itself is negligible, the insulating value depending entirely upon the thickness of the dead air space the material provides. A one-inch dead air space filled with steelwool, for instance, will give the same insulation as a one-inch space filled with down. There are no "miracle" materials.

In camping and climbing equipment there are two distinct functions which insulating materials must serve. The first and most common is the requirement for an insulating material which will compress to the smallest possible volume for packing and which will, on the other hand, expand to the greatest possible volume for insulating when released.

The second function of insulating materials is confined almost exclusively to the bottoms of sleeping bags or the insulating pads which go under them. It requires a material with the opposite characteristics. It must be of low enough density to provide an insulating air space but firm enough to *resist* compression. Obviously a material which compresses easily for packing will also compress under the weight of the body, thus eliminating its insulating value. Conversely, these materials of limited compressibility must be used sparingly since an insulation which won't compress under body weight will not roll into a pack readily. These materials are used as padding under the body at the points of greatest compression—the shoulders, hips, and feet.

DOWN

The natural down from water fowl is the best of all known insulating materials of the easily compressed type—the least weight will fill the greatest volume and will in turn compress to the smallest space for packing. Down can also be tightly compressed for long periods of time and still regain almost one hundred per cent of its volume. Its durability is superior to all other insulation as it can be compressed and expanded over and over again with very little loss in loft.

Down is distinct from feathers, although there are always small feathers mixed with down. A true down pod has no quill whatsoever. It is rather a multitude of light fuzzy filaments extending radially from a central nucleus. The quality of down depends on the size and symmetry of the down pods and upon the absence of feathers, dirt, or other contamination. Goose down is generally superior to duck down because the pods are larger although, as with all natural materials, the quality varies. The quality is usually determined by the filling power and by the amount the down will re-expand after compression. A good grade of goose down will fill about 500 cubic inches per ounce of down.

The Army Quartermaster has vacuum packed down as hard as a rock for years and an hour after release it was back to almost its original volume. Down is used to advantage chiefly in sleeping bags and insulated garments to be used at extremely low temperatures. It is sometimes adulterated with feathers to stretch the supply. Since down is a by-product of the meat packing industry, there is no way to increase the supply to meet the demand unless people will eat more geese.

DACRON BATTING

Dacron batting is next in efficiency to down in the ease with which it can be compressed. A greater weight of Dacron is required to expand it into the same amount of space as down and at the same time it cannot be compressed so compactly as down. After prolonged compression it does not expand to quite its original volume. However, it does have the advantages of being a synthetic and therefore a uniform fiber, inexpensive and readily available. It also retains thickness when wet which is not true of down. It can regain much of its original resiliency by being washed and tumble dried in a home dryer. Dacron must be stitched in bats to hold it in place rather than packed in loose like down; otherwise it will shift and bunch together leaving cold spots in the sleeping bag or garment.

Continuous filament polyester fiberfill insulation, such as Dacron Fiberfill II and PolarGuard, are fine insulators particularly where damp and moisture are encountered. This type of polyester insulation will quickly regain its loft even when damp. It is also relatively inexpensive. These two factors make it a valuable sleeping bag and jacket insulator.

FOAM INSULATION

Foam plastics furnish some of the best materials for the compression resisting function of insulating materials, providing insulation and support for the shoulders, hips, and feet. Weight for weight they will furnish the most support under a sleeping body and hence the most insulation against cold ground and snow. Although these products are very good they are difficult to use for sleeping bags and are best used as a separate pad under the bag.

Table of Support of Various Materials

Support provided by equal weights per area (.1 gm/cm²) under a loading of .5 kg/cm². This represents the approximate practical weight for a sleeping pad and the pressure exerted by body pressure points.

MATERIAL	cm of thickness under load
Spongex 534	.85
Polyurethane Foam	.75
Ensolite M	.70
Virgin wool overlayed with ¼″ Ensolite	.67
Polyester foam	.63
Virgin wool batting	.60
Sponge rubber G-200-C	.55
Dacron batting	.50
Dacron pile fabric	.40
White goose down	.32

Compiled by GERRY for USAF Arctic Aeromedical Lab.

LEATHER

Leather is a complicated subject because it involves more art than science and it is difficult to nail down sources of dependable grade leather. Being a natural product, the quality of leather varies greatly.

Leather is classified in two ways, by the name of the animal it comes from and the type of tanning method used. Because of its general availability steer and cowhide are perhaps the most commonly used of all leathers. They produce heavy, coarse grained leather used for most straps, belts, saddles, harnesses, etc. Those animals growing in warm climates produce leathers of finer grain and more compact structure than those growing in cold climates. Leathers from animals growing in cold climates are generally thicker.

Top grain (the skin side) cowhide is the best grade leather. Straps cut from along the back are firm and tough while leather from the belly is soft and porous. Splits (the inside leather) are the opposite of top grain and are not suitable here.

Calfskins are fine grained, close textured leathers but too light for use except as reinforcing for pack bottoms or rappel patches on pants and jackets. Capeskin can be split down thinner than other leathers and still retain its toughness. It is good for use in mittens, gloves, etc.

Horsehide is good too and cordovan which is cut from the butt of the hide would make excellent straps if it were not for its high cost.

Sheepskin and deerskin are too soft and porous to be of much use for equipment such as this. Fancy leathers such as ostrich, alligator, sharkskin, etc., while having excellent properties, are not of practical value here either.

There are two basic tanning methods, the age old vegetable tanning and the relatively new chrome tanning process. Vegetable tanning is very time consuming, taking from two to six months even by modern processes. This process is essential for the tanning of heavy cowhides—up to a quarter inch in thickness. These cowhides are used for making belting and harness leathers. These leathers are also prestretched and impregnated with oils and grease (curried) to prevent their becoming soft and stretching when wet. Most of these leathers are suitable for pack straps. However, vegetable tanned leathers dry out and become brittle if not properly cared for.

Most of the heavy-appearing uncurried vegetable tanned cowhides are not waterproof. They will become soft and spongy and will stretch entirely out of shape when wet. Many of these leathers are suitable for molding into camera cases and such, but must be protected against future wetting if they are to retain their molded shape. Such leather is not suitable for pack straps unless it is made waterproof and kept that way. Good quality, heavy vegetable tanned leathers are readily available as tooling or carving leather.

Chrome tanning is a much more rapid process. However, it results in a soft leather that is sometimes very spongy. Most light weight skins are tanned by this process and it is very difficult to find chrome tanned leather heavy enough and firm enough for good pack straps. Chrome tanned leathers have the advantage of being naturally waterproof. They will retain their shape even when wet.

Synthetics such as Corfam, Naugahyde, and Aztran now being used in shoes and upholstery are satisfactory, for such applications as reinforcing pack bottoms, but they lack the tensile strength needed for straps.

Leather thickness is described as ounces per square foot. A 7 to 8 ounce leather is heavy enough for pack straps, 5 to 6 ounce for most other uses. 1 to 2 ounce light leather is used for clothing and reinforcing pack bottoms.

Waterproofings such as neat's-foot oil, or greases which are absorbed by leather, will soften it and allow it to stretch unless it is prestretched as in belting and harness leather. Wax type dressings such as ordinary shoe polish don't soak in, give a good repellent surface, but wear off quickly. Satisfactory compromise dressings such as Sno-Seal are made of waxes combined with a solvent which penetrates the leather and evaporates leaving the hard wax behind as a dressing in the surface of the leather.

Some of the silicone compounds are used to great advantage in the tanning and dressing of leather but whether or not the manufacturer has put their advantages to best use can be determined only by testing the specific products. Everything with the word silicone on the label is not necessarily good.

Leather is best cut with a good sharp knife against a board, using a metal straightedge since the blade tends to wander off the desired line. The outline of the piece should be marked in pencil and the straightedge held *very firmly*. Razor blades can be used but unless they are new they won't cut well.

CLOSURES

ZIPPERS

Although there are many sizes, qualities, and makes of zippers, as with everything described, it seems there are only a few applicable to this equipment. There is the light size 3 or 4 and the size which is called either 5 or 6 depending on the manufacturer, and very occasionally the extra large size 7. In addition, these sizes are available in various widths of tapes. The light weight spiral nylon zipper, commonly used on women's clothing, is too delicate for most uses in camping and climbing gear except for mosquito nettings in tents. Here it is convenient to have a pull tab on both sides so the zipper may be pulled from both inside and outside the tent.

Following is a table showing the relative weights per foot and relative strengths for various zippers. The strength per single tooth is an indication of how easily the zipper is damaged by snagging. The spiral coil zippers are superior in this respect.

Table of Zipper Properties
PRESSED ON METAL TEETH

Size	Teeth	Tape	Weight in oz. per foot	Strength across 1" of teeth	Strength per tooth
4	Alum.	7/16"	3/16 oz.	82 lbs.	8 lbs. pulled off
6	Alum.	9/16"	5/16 oz.	105 lbs.	8 lbs. pulled off
6	Brass	9/16"	10/16 oz.	128 lbs.	19 lbs. pulled off
9	Alum.	9/16"	9/16 oz.	173 lbs.	
9	Brass	12/16"	26/16 oz.	336 lbs.	

DIE CAST METAL TEETH

Size	Teeth	Tape	Weight in oz. per foot	Strength across 1" of teeth	Strength per tooth
5	Cast	5/"	9/16 oz.	100 lbs.	20 lbs. no damage

Table of Zipper Properties (cont.)

Size	Teeth	Tape	Weight in oz. per foot	Strength across 1" of teeth	Strength per tooth
7	Cast	3/4"	20/16 oz. (1 1/4 oz.)	250 lbs.	

NYLON ZIPPERS

Size	Teeth	Tape	Weight in oz. per foot	Strength across 1" of teeth	Strength per tooth
7	Molded	3/4"	6/16 oz.	200 lbs.	20 lbs.

NYLON COIL ZIPPERS

Size	Teeth	Tape	Weight in oz. per foot	Strength across 1" of teeth	Strength per tooth
5	Coil	9/16"	6/16 oz.	200 lbs.	N/A°
7	Coil	10/16"	8/16 oz.	216 lbs.	N/A
10	Coil	10/16"	15/16 oz.	314 lbs.	N/A

°Coil zippers do not fail across the teeth in a manner comparable to toothed zippers. Even damaged coils are operable.

The large size zipper, 5 or 6, is the zipper commonly used on jackets and heavy clothing. These zippers are available with either heavy or light weight tapes for use with heavy or light fabrics. They are suitable for most of the uses described, sleeping bags, tents, clothing, and packs.

There are many recent developments in zippers with features desirable for camping equipment use. Greatest durability is given by those with teeth die cast onto the tape such as Coats & Clark and Crown zippers in metal and Waldes in nylon. The Waldes size 8800 is very large and virtually snag proof yet weighs less than a size 5 metal zipper. Coats & Clark are available in "Wing Sweep" which features a ridge of metal on the teeth for the slider to rub against instead of the tape. The most common failure of a zipper is to have just one tooth get pulled out of line. Die cast teeth actually become welded to the tape and cannot be moved without tearing away the tape itself.

Zippers that open and close in either direction are rather common now and some offer this feature in a jacket zipper. This means that there are two sliders on the zipper, opening from either the top or the bottom. You can open it from the bottom for sitting in a car, or run both sliders together at the waist to hold it around you but otherwise open for ventilation. This type zipper also has an advantage for zip-together sleeping bags. You can open the bag at the foot for ventilation on hot summer nights.

Two sizes of nylon coil zippers have applications in tents, clothing, sleeping bags and packs. They have several obvious advantages, the most important being that a break can be "healed" by passing the slider over the area. The coil zipper is tighter, allowing less cold air to pass through.

Coil separating zippers are somewhat more difficult to start and some have relatively stiff operation, but they are light and durable.

Zippers may be repaired or revised by changing their lengths as long as the teeth are in perfect working order. One or two teeth out of line will ruin a zipper and make it worthless. The easiest method of shortening a zipper is to cut it off at the top or open end and pull off several teeth from each side. If the top stops cannot be pried open and pressed on the tape again above the teeth, satisfactory top stops can be made with needle and thread by whipping over and over between the last two teeth on each side of the top opening.

In replacing a damaged slider it is easiest to remove the two top stops, slide off the damaged slider, and replace it with a new slider at the top. Make certain that the zipper stays closed during this operation! Occasionally a toothed zipper will open behind the slider. The quickest way to repair the zipper if this happens is to remove the top stops, run the slider off, remove the bottom stop and start the slider on again from the bottom. As soon as the slider is on and the first few closed teeth appear, the bottom stop should be replaced. However, most bottom stops cannot be used a second time and a new one will have to be put on. The best type of bottom stop is one that fits over the teeth and has long prongs to go through the tape to be clinched on the back side. A temporary repair can be made by sewing the bottom tightly together with thread, but this does not wear well and the teeth will frequently get out of alignment. If there is much zipper work to be done a few dozen top and bottom stops can be purchased from a zipper repair shop.

When the tape around the separating fixture of a zipper, such as is commonly used on jackets, becomes worn or the fixture itself becomes bent, it is practically impossible to fix it. Such a zipper should be replaced.

There are various types of zipper sliders. A non-locking slider will slide down the tape and open by itself when pressure is applied. These should not be used on clothing or duffel bags.

There are three types of locking sliders. They must be used with discretion since the locking mechanism transfers all the force of the pull to one or two zipper teeth. It is sometimes better to use a non-locking slider which will open under stress rather than a locking slider which will ruin an entire zipper if enough force is applied to deform a tooth. Coats & Clark die-cast zippers are more able to take this strain than most. For instance, the zipper in a tent door could be damaged when the strain is applied on a locking slider by someone stepping on a half opened door. The notch-lock slider has a small projection inside which will catch on the tooth when force is applied to separate the tapes, but will run freely at all other times.

The pin-lock slider used mostly on pants flies has a pin attached to the pull tab which engages the teeth when the tab is folded flat against the slider. This lock is easily removed if it is not wanted.

The spring-lock slider is the most common type for the large size zippers. This lock allows the slider to move only when the tab is pulled out away from the zipper chain. This lock has the advantage of engaging two teeth instead of one. For tents and sleeping bags where access is had to both sides of the zipper, a slider with a pull tab on both sides is necessary.

Sliders with little chains and rings are easier to grasp than the slider tab itself. Where it is necessary to use a zipper with mittens the pull tab should have a large enough hole to receive a long leather thong. Some sliders do not have holes big enough to put anything through, let alone a leather thong.

Where necessary a zipper can be made fairly water repellent by treating the tape with any commercial repellent. If this is a wax or silicone treatment it also helps the zipper slide easily. Sticky zippers can sometimes be helped by rubbing with wax.

VELCRO TAPE

Velcro tape is a closing device that has some uses similar to zippers. It consists of two different woven nylon tapes. One tape is composed of tiny loops like miniature terry cloth loops. The other is a mass of little hooks like a cocklebur. When these two tapes are pressed together they cling tenaciously and have to be peeled apart. The tape is both washable and sewable. One good use which has been developed for this kind of tape is the closure of down items. It is sewn along the opening, with snaps set at intervals, making a good draft free and snag proof closing which doesn't flatten out the insulation. Other uses are being developed. Beware the hot iron! It will melt the tape. Velcro is hard on cold hands—design carefully.

SNAPS

Snaps, of course, have many uses on closures. The most common snaps available are Laundry Proof Snappers. Available in inexpensive home setting kits at sewing centers, these snaps hold well, much better than glove or birdcage snaps which are sold in craft shops. For heavy duty a Durable Dot Fastener or similar snap can be applied at luggage shops, tent and awning makers, or makers of convertible car tops. Car top or slip cover manufacturers are also likely to have Lift Dot and other types of fasteners designed for specific purposes. Fairly inexpensive hand set tools for Durable Dot Snaps are available in craft shops if much snap work is to be done.

HARDWARE

The very best hardware for climbing and camping gear is, of course, non-rusting and corrosion resistant. Steel is often used with plating of one sort or another to protect it against rusting. This is not very satisfactory. Equipment such as this gets hard wear and the plating is eventually scratched and worn through leaving the steel open to rust. Hardware made of non-rusting metals such as brass, zinc, copper, aluminum, and stainless steel provides insurance against rust. Brass and copper are sometimes nickel plated to prevent corrosion in a salty atmosphere and to put a polish on the hardware for appearance.

BUCKLES

Buckles are used in climbing and camping equipment primarily for making pack straps adjustable. They are also used for clothing straps and straps for general packing.

The tongue buckle is the most common but has the disadvantage of being adjustable only where the holes are placed in the strap and of concentrating the strain on the one small hole in the strap.

The web strap buckle is a buckle with serrated teeth gripping the full width of the strap and holding any position along the strap. This buckle can also be used for leather straps if the leather is of uniform thickness. There must be some slack in the strap for unfastening this buckle. Under some circumstances it is very difficult to obtain enough slack to unfasten it.

There are several types of special buckles which are operable under load or with mittens. These may be useful under certain conditions, such as extreme cold when fingers might be frostbitten if mittens were removed, or with a very tight pack or roll where it is extremely difficult to get sufficient slack to release the usual buckle. Examples of such special buckles are the skate strap buckle and tourniquet buckles.

For straps which do not require frequent adjustment, such as shoulder straps on packs, a very satisfactory type is the army ladder buckle which depends entirely on friction. Threaded one way this is also an easily released buckle but will not hold much load. Threaded for maximum friction it is very secure.

RIVETS

Rivets are used mainly for fastening leather straps and fastening hardware onto the straps. They may be used to reinforce the attachment of leather to fabric, but for this purpose they should never be used alone for they concentrate too much strain on one place in the fabric. When being used with fabric a rivet should always be used with stitching, the rivet being set just inside the stitching. The stitching then accepts the strain first and distributes it. The rivet takes only the strain the stitching gives up by its elasticity. Preferably the rivet should be backed on the fabric side by a small piece of leather. One good rivet in a ¾″ wide firm chrome leather strap can support approximately 90 pounds.

A rivet which is easy to use and at the same time gives the greatest strength is a copper rivet and burr. This rivet has a large head, and a burr or washer is placed over the other end before it is peened over. A hole must be made in the material to receive the rivet.

The Dot Speedy Rivet is not as strong as a copper rivet and burr but is easier to use. The two parts are simply driven together with a hammer. These also require a hole in the material before setting.

A tubular rivet can be driven through the material and set in one operation using a cheap tool generally available at hardware stores. The set is accomplished by splaying the tubular end in a star shape. If used with fabric it must be backed by a leather washer.

MISCELLANEOUS HARDWARE

There are occasional uses for other items of harness, boot, and bag hardware such as dee rings, snap hooks, strap tips, lacing hooks and eyelets, grommets, and washers and snaps.

The strongest type of dee rings are cast in one piece or bent from wire and welded. If they are bent and not welded they may pull apart. Square corners prevent their turning in the strap. Cast zinc dee rings are malleable and will not break.

There are many types of snap hooks available, cast, stamped out, and formed of wire. Some are large enough to work with mittens on the hands and some are too small to work comfortably at all.

Strap tips are used on web strap ends to prevent fraying. Horseshoe style tips are almost impossible to set without tools as they tend to spread too wide for the buckle when compressed onto the strap. Ferrule style tips (a brass cup) are easy to pound flat on the strap. Another tip which is easy to use is a simple fold of metal with teeth to grip the strap. This is pounded together over the end of the strap.

All of the hardware mentioned can usually be obtained at hardware and luggage stores, or if there is still a harness and saddle shop convenient, all these items and many more of interest will be found.

Lacing hooks, such as are used on boots and shoes, and shoe lacing eyelets are useful items that can be purchased and applied at shoe repair shops. Stationery stores can supply relatively inexpensive hand tools for setting eyelets. Larger size holes require grommets and washers which are available at tent and awning manufacturers. These may also be set with an inexpensive hand tool which would be convenient to acquire if much equipment is to be made or repaired.

WATER REPELLENTS

There are no truly permanent water repellents. Even the "durable" water repellents will wear out after exposure to the weather so our main concern will be with repellents of the non-durable types. The durable repellents have to be factory applied to the fabric before it is made up. The non-durable types, though they wash out with a single laundering or cleaning can be readily reapplied at home.

Since most items of equipment come treated with one of the durable repellents, the proper care and maintenance of this finish rates first consideration. First of all, there is considerable variation in the effectiveness of the treatment even when it is done to government specifications. Secondly, dirt is the great enemy of water repellent finishes but the durable ones can be rejuvenated by proper cleaning. The usual dry cleaners' solvent contains oil soluble detergents and spotting agents which destroy the repellency. For this reason only pure solvent must be used. Pure Stoddard's solvent is available for the home cleaning job to make sure it is done properly. If the item is washed, only a mild soap, not a detergent, should be used. The item should be agitated as little as possible and it should be rinsed two or three times in clean water. Whether cleaned or washed, ironing with a hot iron for several minutes will do much to restore the repellency.

Now let us assume that the original repellency has gone. This happens rather rapidly with nylon fabrics, especially those exposed to sunlight at high altitudes. By far the most convenient way to replace the repellency is with one of the aerosol cans of repellent. This is easy enough to do several times a summer in the case of a jacket. A tent should last most of the season with one application unless it is left up. The repellent is probably good for 2 continuous weeks out in the weather. Before applying any repellent, the item must be clean and thoroughly rinsed free of any soap or detergent.

A dry cleaner can apply repellent to uninsulated clothing. However, dry cleaners usually apply the repellent by immersing the garment in the solution so if it is a down jacket or sleeping bag, the down will pick up the repellent and lose a good deal of its loft. Down or Dacron insulated items should have the repellent applied to the outer surface only.

In the final analysis, the best possible method of rain proofing either your clothing or your tent is to use a very light plastic coated outer shell over a breathable inner fabric with plenty of air circulation between. Of course on damp days you don't want to be in your poncho every time it sprinkles. Outer clothing should be water repellent for maximum convenience.

Pack sacks are one thing that can be made waterproof by plastic coating the fabric.

The above treatments are for tent, pack, and wind clothing fabrics of cotton, Orlon, or nylon. It is also possible to apply a fairly durable repellent treatment to wool which can be renewed after each washing by using aluminum sulfate. The following was one of the oldest non-durable treatments for cottons but poor performance caused it to fall into disuse until research for the Army Quartermaster rediscovered it as a permanent finish for woolens. The wool fabric is first impregnated for 10–15 minutes with a 0.25% mild soap solution at 100°F and then squeezed out. While still wet it is placed in a 0.1% solution of aluminum sulfate at 135° to 140°F and worked for 15 minutes. It is then removed and allowed to dry. Hard water is detrimental to this treatment. To renew the repellency after subsequent washings in mild soap it is only necessary to add the aluminum sulfate to the rinse water.

There are several other factors beside the treatment technique which affect the repellency of the fabric. One of these is the tightness of the fabric. A fabric with a high porosity cannot be made as repellent as a good closely woven fabric. Thick fabrics are much more resistant to moisture than thin ones, but this of course means added weight. Using two layers of fabric, such as in tent flies and double panels in clothing, can increase the total repellency tremendously—up to 100 times that of a single layer of the same fabric. Thus there is good reason for double shoulders and other selected portions of outer clothing and for rain flies for tents.

Repellency is measured in several ways and all of them anticipate an eventual soaking through. Any fabric that is permeable to air and only repellent to water is going to soak through eventually. If the fabric is being worked and rubbed continually the water will soak through sooner than if it is left undisturbed. If the fabric is stretched tight or backed by a hard, non-resilient surface it will soak through sooner than if it has a little give to it. If it is dirty it will soak through sooner than if it is clean. Don't expect the impossible, especially from the extremely light weight fabrics.

SOURCES

Here is a list of sources of supply for the materials described.

Frostline, Box 589, Broomfield, Colorado, 80020
Holubar Mountain Equipment, P.O. Box 7, Boulder, Colorado, 80302

Recreational Equipment, Inc., 1525 11th Avenue, Seattle, Washington, 98122

The Ski Hut, 1615 University Avenue, Berkeley, California, 94703

Montgomery Ward

Penney's

Sears Roebuck

Tent and awning suppliers, yard goods shops, leather wholesalers, luggage shops, marine outfitters, sailmakers, shoe manufacturers and repair shops, harness and saddle shops, mattress and bedding manufacturers, army surplus stores, hardware stores, drygoods departments, handicraft shops, notions departments.

The consumer should be aware that all commercially manufactured tents have been required to meet federal flammability standards since 1975, and it is likely that standards will be developed for other products. Ask suppliers if the fabrics you are considering meet these standards.

Grommets and washers can sometimes be set in your own items by local Tent and Awning Suppliers, Sailmakers, or Luggage Shops. Rivets can sometimes be set by Harness and Saddle Shops, Luggage Shops, Shoe Repair Shops. Heavy duty snaps such as Durable Dots or Lift Dots can usually be purchased and set for you at Tent and Awning Suppliers, Luggage Shops, or Convertible Car Top Shops.

Plastics can be supplied by handicraft or plastics shops, marine outfitters (boat covering kits), Sears Roebuck (boat covering kits), Montgomery Ward (boat covering kits).

CHAPTER III PATTERNS AND SEWING

One of the jobs of this book is to make it possible for anyone with normal dexterity to construct the basic gear for backpacking. It would be foolish to say it's all easy. It isn't. The secret is in the planning. Before actual construction of any item begins, the project must be understood, carefully planned, and laid out. If these preliminary steps are bypassed or skimmed over, discouraging difficulties may arise later on. This chapter will help with the careful planning necessary for success. No great skill is required—but a lot of patience is. One of the great virtues of sewing is that it can be ripped out and done again if a mistake is made.

There will be detailed dimensional drawings, step-by-step instructions and complete materials lists for a few of the most generally useful items of equipment and in addition there will be a complete discussion of design considerations, materials, and construction details for each type of gear. The aim is to present the problems involved and to help the reader become familiar with the performance required of his equipment. He will eventually be able to design equipment to suit his particular needs. This can provide him with the best possible equipment available anywhere.

LAYOUTS AND CUTTING

The patterns for all the small items of equipment such as clothing and packs can be laid out on a good sized table. The materials for large pieces of equipment such as tents and sleeping bags should be laid out on the floor—preferably away from cats and small children, although this difficulty seems to be a standard hazard. Occasionally a sleeping bag can be laid out on a very large table.

A paper pattern should be cut out for all the more complicated shapes, including clothing and some of the packs. By careful measuring, chalk marks can be laid out directly on the fabric for the more rectangular packs, tents, and sleeping bags.

Drawings of the more complicated pieces are marked off in squares to make it easier to transfer the exact outline to the full size required for the project.

A large sheet of wrapping paper should be marked off in squares of the size indicated in the drawing. It will be a simple matter to transfer the rectangular shapes to the large paper. For the curved and complicated outlines the technique is to notice where the outline crosses the various squares on the scale drawing and to copy this carefully onto the squared paper so the outline crosses the squares in the same proportion. It is a help to take a straight edged piece of cardboard and near one end mark off the length of one side of a square on the small drawing and divide this into eight equal parts. Near the other end lay off the length of the side of one square of the large drawing and divide this also into eight equal parts. Using these two scales on their respective drawings it will be easy to measure the spot at which the outline crosses each square and precisely transfer these intersections from the small to the large drawing.

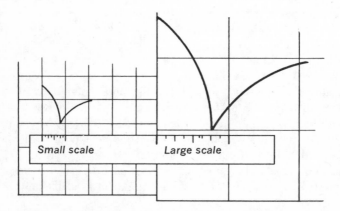

Small scale   Large scale

The parts for most of the packs can be marked off directly onto the fabric. The parts should be nested for the most economical cutting. Intelligent use can be made of the selvedge so that it falls where it is desirable to have a non-fraying edge.

The large pieces of tents and sleeping bags must sometimes be roughed out first. Pieces are sewn together to form a blank of the approximate outline, large enough on which to lay out the exact outline. Such a pieced seam should be a flat felled seam, and in the case of tents it should be felled like a shingle to shed the water. These large pieces must be carefully cut to take advantage of the fact that most patterns are symmetrical. The remaining angle left from each piece cut on a particular angle can be reversed forming the correct angle for one side of the corresponding piece on the other side. This is only true of reversible fabrics. This foresight and planning saves yards of material which would otherwise be wasted.

A mistake in cutting is not an irrevocable catastrophe. The fabric can always be pieced together with neat felled seams and cut again.

A tailor's chalk or wax marking crayon should be used for all marks. Chalk will rub off when the marks are no longer needed and the crayon marks can be melted out with a warm iron. If the material is to be handled much during construction crayon will stick longer.

A yardstick of the kind given free by lumber companies is essential. An 8-foot steel tape is very handy for the larger pieces. A very satisfactory 8-foot straightedge can be made from a piece of lattice selected for straightness from a local lumber company. This can be used for laying out pieces too long for the yardstick.

A good pair of long bladed shears can be used for all cutting. Pinking shears may come in especially handy for clothing.

Cut edges of nylon must always be treated to prevent fraying. If finished seams of some sort are used, or if the seams are bound with tape so that no raw edges are left exposed in the completed item the nylon can be left as cut. Otherwise when exposed edges are left they can be secured against fraying by melting them very slightly in the flame of a candle. If pinking shears are used the ends of the pinks can be melted very quickly in a flame.

How to sear: Place a candle in a holder on a solid surface, such as a table. Do not lean your head over the flame. Hold the edge of the fabric tightly between your hands and pass it close to (but not directly in) the flame. Melt the very fuzzy edge of the fabric—not the fabric itself. Very rarely will the fabric catch on fire. It burns with an almost invisible flame that you may not even notice. If this should happen you can easily blow it out or pinch it out with your fingers. Continue to hold the fabric taut until it cools (2 or 3 seconds), or the edge may shrink.

SEWING

It might be a great help for the novice to obtain a good basic book on sewing and read it through to learn the terms and basic information offered there. Many of the techniques are applicable to this equipment (and will give assurance as well as added information).

A sewing machine is almost essential for tents, sleeping bags, and clothing due to the great number of seams. However, packs can be sewn by hand. If a sewing machine is not available at home and one of the long-seam projects is planned, it is a good idea to rent one. Good machines are generally available for rent at local sewing centers. The lockstitch machine, the seams of which will not pull out, is better than the chainstitch machine. The rotary bobbin will sew faster than the long shuttle type. Even though a machine is used, some difficult-to-reach spots may have to be sewn by hand. For this type of work a couple of sturdy needles and a thimble will do the job, or a sailmaker's palm can be used to sew the heaviest materials. For hand sewing a little beeswax will not only strengthen the thread but will help prevent nylon thread from kinking.

All of these projects have been made on home sewing machines; sometimes with difficulty but most times easily with patience. There is tremendous variation in sewing machines, even of the same make and year, after a year or two of use. It should be emphasized that the machine should be in good working order! Frequently a machine will have minor troubles which go unnoticed with ordinary sewing, or cause only minor inconvenience. These faults should be corrected before beginning the equipment projects in this book. It is also important to understand how a machine works. Patience and practice in technique will usually result in a job done well.

As we have mentioned before, some trouble may be encountered in using nylon or other synthetic thread in a sewing machine, and it will help to understand the operation of the machine. On one side of the needle there is a long groove. On the opposite side near the eye there is a depression. As the needle penetrates the material on the downstroke it will drag the thread along with it. As soon as the needle starts back up again, the thread lying in the groove will come up with the needle, but the thread on the opposite side, having no groove to lie in, will stick against the material. This action forms a small loop of thread alongside the needle which the sewing hook in a rotary bobbin machine, or the point of the shuttle in a shuttle machine, will pick up and pass around the bobbin case to form the lockstitch. The synthetic threads, especially nylon, are so elastic that they will stretch considerably on the downstroke and will snap back at the beginning of the upstroke, forming no loop for the hook to pick up. This causes the familiar dropped stitch when the machine refuses to sew. At other times the loop is only partly formed and the sewing hook neatly splits the thread causing an even worse mess.

Several things can be done to remedy this difficulty. First, an extra large needle can be used to make a large hole and reduce the friction against the thread on the downstroke. In leather and other dense non-woven materials a chisel point needle may be used which will actually cut through the material rather than merely push it aside as a regular needle does. Regular needles can be ground to a chisel point on an oilstone. All this tends to reduce the friction against the thread on the downstroke thus reducing the stretching.

Second, thread tensions may be loosened as far as possible thus reducing the amount of stretching on the downstroke. Great care must be used in adjusting the bobbin tension since a fraction of a turn on the tension screw will make an appreciable difference. The top tension should then be adjusted to match the bobbin. Sewing a practice scrap will show whether the tensions are evenly adjusted. They should sew a stitch which is the same on either side of the material. If one tension is tighter than the other it will pull the thread through to that side and produce an irregular looking seam.

When the going gets too heavy for the machine, the flywheel may be slowly turned by hand making one stitch at a time. Some surprisingly thick materials can be sewn in this manner. It is important to go very slowly after the needle has entered the material until it is well on its way back up again. This allows the sewing hook to catch on the loop of thread.

One good stitch for hand sewing is illustrated. This backstitch gives a good strong continuous seam.

For sewing leather and other material too heavy for the machine a stitching awl is recommended. A stitching awl is a small hand tool which produces a lockstitch as the machine does but which uses a very heavy thread and a very sharp edged needle which can be pushed through almost any material. These awls are usually equipped with several needles including a curved one which can be used for stitching when it is impossible to sew from both sides of the material.

Following are descriptions of general sewing terms which will be used throughout the book, and general instructions for items which are used with several pieces of gear.

PLAIN SEAM

Match the edges to be joined, right sides together, and stitch once about ¼″ in from the edge and a second time about ⅛″ in to retard raveling. This seam is used only where the wrong side will not be exposed or in packs where the heavy fabric prevents a more finished seam. This same seam can be bound with seam binding the second time around to give a more finished appearance and complete security against raveling.

HEM SEAM

This seam is similar to the plain seam except that the edges are folded over before stitching. They are folded either once (rough hem seam)

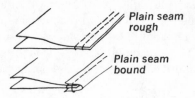

or twice (finished hem seam) and this is used to join light fabrics such as in sleeping bags to prevent down going through the seams, or where a finished seam is wanted with a minimum of needle holes such as in a coated fabric tarp.

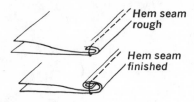

FLAT FELLED SEAM

This is a common dressmaking seam and the one used most often in camping equipment and clothes. However, we generally make the seam inside out so it is felled up on the inside. This gives fewer stitches on the outside of tents and the fabric laps like a shingle so it will shed water. The first step is to match the edges to be joined, right sides together, and stitch $\frac{1}{2}''$ on from the edge. Next, if the fabric is heavy, the direction of the fell is decided and the underneath flap trimmed to half its width. If the fabric is light there is no need to bother with trimming. Finally, fold the flap of the fabric over and stitch down. A rough felled seam has this folded just once and is used where extremely heavy fabrics are encountered or often just for an inch or so when one felled seam crosses another making too many layers for easy stitching. A finished felled seam is folded twice so all rough edges are covered.

TOP STITCHED SEAM

This seam is used to sew outside pockets, etc., to packs. It eliminates the need for sewing inside the pocket and yet it provides an inside edge that can't ravel past the first stitching. Though usually left rough, this can also be finished by folding the edge one more time and allowing an extra $\frac{1}{4}''$ for this in cutting.

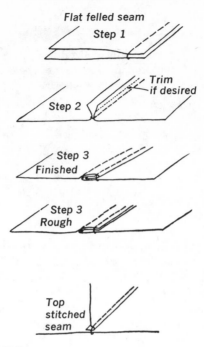

Flat felled seam

Step 1

Step 2

Trim if desired

Step 3
Finished

Step 3
Rough

Top
stitched
seam

INSERTION SEAM

Often there is a double piece of fabric to be joined to a single piece. This is done by matching all the edges to be joined with the double pieces on the outsides, right sides together, and sewing in about ⅜″ from the edges. The outside pieces are then folded back away from the inserted piece, aligned with each other, pulled tight against the first stitched seam and then stitched together ¼″ from the original seam. Sometimes double pieces are joined at each side to a single piece. The first side is easy to do but the second side requires all the rest of the item to be stuffed between the double pieces for the first stitch. With the light fabrics used for this equipment this can usually be done without trouble.

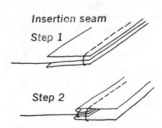

Insertion seam

Step 1

Step 2

PLAIN HEM

This hem is used to provide a clean edge to any piece of fabric not sewn to something else. The width of the hem is its finished width and in most cases there will be two folds to produce a finished hem with no raw edges. Occasionally a rough hem will be used in leather or coated fabrics, or with a selvedge that can't fray, and these are folded only once.

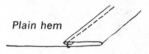

Plain hem

DRAWHEMS

A plain hem can often be used to contain a drawstring but it is often necessary to install a hem for a drawstring in the center of a piece such as at the waist of a parka. This hem is made of a strip of fabric at least 1½" wide, pieced to length if necessary. Sew the first edge inside out, then fold the second edge and stitch down. A drawhem is often needed around a parka face opening or cuffs and these are finished off with a facing type of hem which must be cut at least 2½" wide. First place right side of the facing against the right side of the opening, edges matching, and sew around ¼" in. Then fold the facing strip around against the inside, being careful that it lies flat, and top stitch it slightly out from the first seam. This facing is often used without any drawstring just to finish off a rough opening. In all cases, if the ends of the drawhems will be exposed, fold over several times before stitching the first time.

Waist drawhem

Facing drawhem

Step 1

Step 2

There are several ways of mounting zippers according to their use. It is better to illustrate these than to try to explain them. Refer to Figs. 1 to 5, Plate I. One point to remember is always to have the zipper on top of the fabric when machine sewing to prevent puckering the zipper. The length of a zipper is measured by the total length of metal including the end stops. In time a zipper can be sewn without pinning, but it is easier at first to press the folded edges of a slot first and pin the zipper in exactly as it is to be. In all cases where fabric flaps cover the zipper, these are folded and sewn to the zipper before installing.

WEB STRAPS

Web, unlike leather, cannot be cut to shape without fraying so some means is needed to taper the ends of wide straps to receive the hardware that attaches them to the narrow straps. Soft webbing can simply be folded over at the corners as in Fig. 6, Plate I, and the hardware attached with a short length of the narrow web. A longer and neater taper can be made by first cutting a Vee in the end of the strap, Fig. 7, Plate I, and sewing this together. Then cover the stitching with a piece of the narrow webbing that also holds the hardware.

PLATE I

Zipper Installation Details

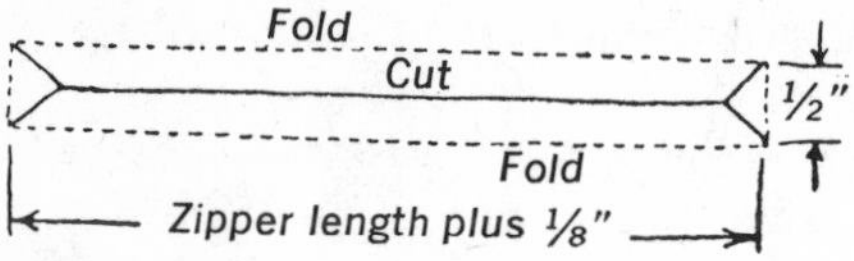

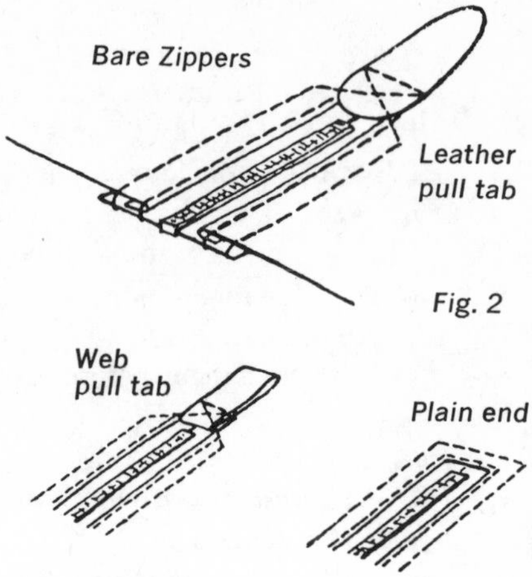

Bare Zippers

Leather
pull tab

Fig. 1

Method of cutting slit for zipper

Fold

Cut

$\frac{1}{2}$"

Fold

Zipper length plus $\frac{1}{8}$"

Fig. 2

Web
pull tab

Plain end

Fig. 3

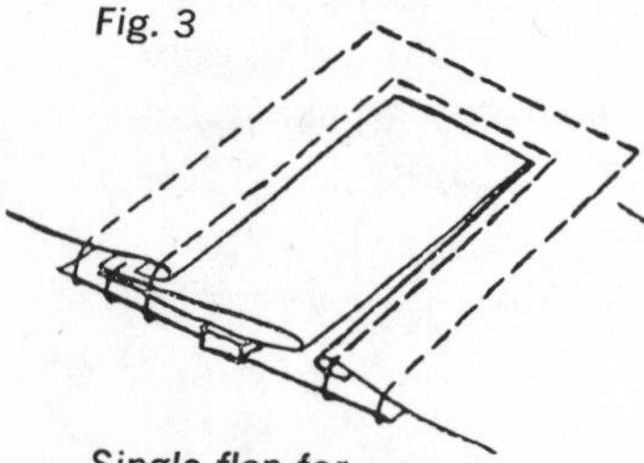

Single flap for
horizontal openings

Fig. 4

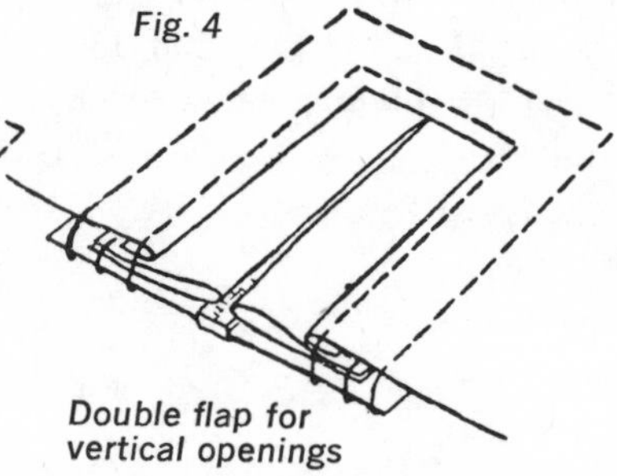

Double flap for
vertical openings

Fig. 5

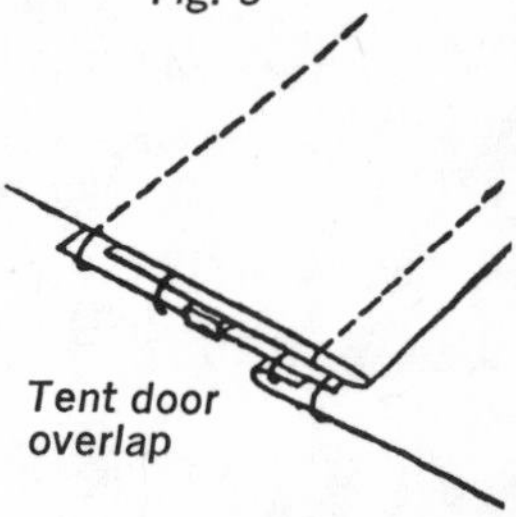

Tent door
overlap

Tapering Web Straps

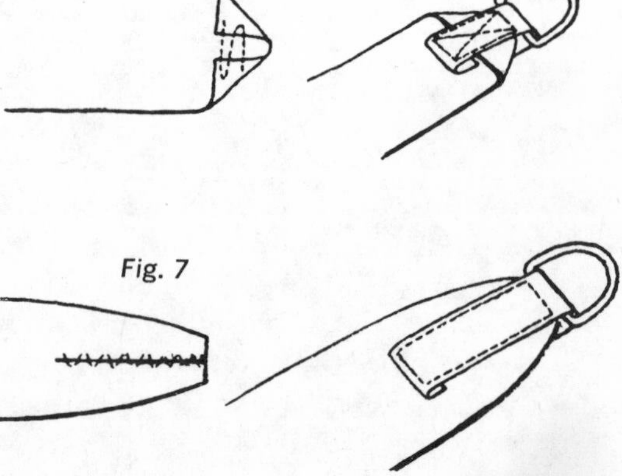

Fig. 6

Fig. 7

CHAPTER IV PACKS

In making a backpacking outfit the pack is a good place to start. In it go most of the other items of equipment and whether they are light or heavy they *have* to be carried on the *back!* An uncomfortable pack has ruined many an otherwise pleasant trip. It stands to reason, therefore, that the best possible planning and design considerations should go into this pivotal piece of equipment.

Back packs fall into three categories: the small frameless sack type; the rucksack type with a frame but designed to hang away from the back; and the pack board type which is designed to be supported on the back.

A thing to be remembered about every pack is that when it is stuffed with a sleeping bag and other equipment it tends to assume a cylindrical shape unless it is restrained. Any simple sack stuffed to overflowing will become as round as a small beer keg and it will be just as uncomfortable on the back. For this reason it is always a good idea to have a pack slightly larger than is actually needed so that it needn't be *stuffed.*

There is only one way to force the small frameless pack to keep its shape—by the use of partitions. This prevents the pack from bulging and at the same time divides it into convenient compartments. This type of frameless pack has to be very carefully packed to prevent cans, crampons, and such hard things from digging into the back. For this reason it is now generally reserved for the light loads required on one-day trips.

The introduction of the frame rucksack in Europe represented an effort to produce a more comfortable pack. The frame served the triple purpose of keeping the shape of the pack despite the load, keeping the load off the wearer's back, and allowing air circulation next to the back for coolness.

For light loads the conventional frame rucksack such as the original Bergen from Norway has the one cardinal advantage of a low center of gravity which makes it a very comfortable pack for climbing and skiing. Due to its numerous pockets and compartments it is also very convenient to use. Most people will find, however, that it has a definite weight limit. It is designed so that the top of the sack hangs away from the back. This creates a backward pull on the shoulders! With loads over twenty pounds, depending on the weight of the person carrying the load, this backward pull is very uncomfortable and the energy expended in resisting it is needlessly wasted. (The heavier the person the heavier the load he can carry this way.)

Heavier loads are more comfortably carried supported on the back with the center of gravity over the hips. For this purpose a pack board frame, with an attached sack should be used.

Fig. 1, Plate II, p. 52, shows the forward lean required for various types of load. These are tracings from photographs. Not only your comfort, but the amount of energy you waste depends on how much you have to lean forward to balance the load over your feet. The straighter you stand the more comfortable you are and the less energy you waste. With a canoe you are standing straight and wasting none of your energy.

A pack board frame can be made more comfortable by a fabric panel or several wide bands which will support the load along the length of the back and not just the lower part. The sack itself is cut so that the load is held close to the back and stacked rather high so that with a slight forward lean of the body the center of gravity of the load is placed directly over the hips. This tends to tip the top of the pack forward onto the back in contrast to the action of the rucksack, the top of which hangs away from the back. Too high a load exerts considerable leverage against the body's natural balance and can be tiring for anything except straight walking.

In addition, placement of the straps and everything else possible is done to increase the tendency to tip the load forward. However, it must be realized that improper pack board packing can also make the pack pull backward on the shoulders as badly as any rucksack. The load must be close to the body and relatively high to fully utilize the efficiency of the pack board design.

Most present-day pack frames have abandoned the "hang it on the shoulders" theory in favor of the "shoulder squeeze." This simply means that the shoulder straps are attached above the level of the shoulders, and a tightly laced back-band is placed across the frame where the curve of the back contacts it. The result is that the shoulders are squeezed, front and back, between the shoulder straps and the upper back-band. This eliminates the backward pull of straps that go up and over the shoulders and partway down the back again.

Much progress has been made recently in hip carrying systems. Originally a simple wide waist belt pulled the lower back-band in to the slope of your buttocks so much of the load was carried there. Then a full circular, padded waist belt made its appearance. This was eventually conically shaped to wedge down over the hips more comfortably, and horns were added to the frame to bring the point of attachment up to the center of the body. Unfortunately, because the center of gravity stayed behind where it was, these horns tend to tip the pack backwards. If the major part of the weight is indeed being carried on the hips, this backward pull is minimal, but if the system is not functioning as intended, this pull can be the cause of some discomfort.

A hip carrying system is not for everyone, but even if you can't use it one hundred per cent of the time, it is a great way to give your shoulders a walking break on a long trip and it should be part of every heavy load carrying system.

There are factors other than weight limits to be considered in the choice of a pack. For instance, for a one-day trip the load will be light and an inexpensive frameless sack can be used. If this sack is compartmented it will be more comfortable because it will hold its shape well, and it will be easier to find your belongings.

For longer trips pack boards with sacks become necessary. The sack will be more convenient if it has the outside pockets of the rucksack for ease in reaching small items. The large capacity of the main sack will take care of the extra food needed on longer trips. A new design, made up of horizontal zippered compartments not only gives the convenience of pockets but allows you to balance your load properly for the conditions encountered. For example the light but bulky sleeping bag can go at the bottom and the heavy compact tent can go in the top compartment where it will stay even though the rest of the pack is empty.

Some packs in this size range are built to carry the load high over the shoulders. This is fine for trails, open terrain, and glacier packing; however the center of gravity is not only a little too high for comfortable climbing but the pack tends to limit the head's backward movement. This stymies the climber who can't lean backward to see above.

In large scale expedition work where a lot of miscellaneous gear must be packed, a large pack board with generous lashing hooks and a shelf at the bottom is necessary. Here again in open terrain a board on which the load can be stacked high over the shoulders is fine. For bushwhacking or difficult climbing a board with a lower center of gravity is necessary. It is a good idea to have a detachable sack for such a pack board. Where necessary this can carry personal gear leaving the pack board completely free for cases of food, cans of gasoline, and bulky equipment. Another weight saving feature is the attachment of shoulder straps to the sack so it can be used alone as a one-day pack.

One very specialized pack is the ski pack, designed especially to carry a pair of skis. Skis, off the feet, are about the most miserable pieces of equipment ever thought up for backpacking. Ski packs are designed with a space behind the side pockets through which the tails of the skis are passed. By strapping the ski tips together a fairly rigid "A" is formed—

PLATE II

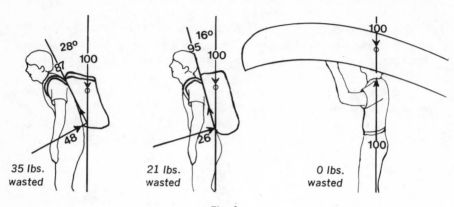

35 lbs.
wasted

21 lbs.
wasted

0 lbs.
wasted

Fig. 1

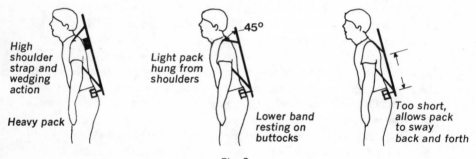

High
shoulder
strap and
wedging
action

Heavy pack

Light pack
hung from
shoulders

Lower band
resting on
buttocks

45°

Too short,
allows pack
to sway
back and forth

Fig. 2

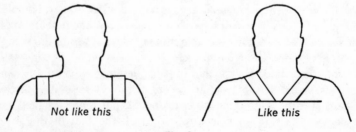

Not like this

Like this

Fig. 3

probably the least inconvenient way to carry them. Fig. 9, Plate IV, p. 59, illustrates a type of ski carrier that can be added to any pack.

To be comfortable the pack should fit the person carrying it. It is often difficult to get a well fitted pack in the desired design from the usual manufacturers, though several make them in various sizes. One good reason for making a pack is that it can be custom tailored. In beginning a pack design it should be borne in mind that the load should not extend out too far from the back. The width of the pack can vary most but should not be too wide or the elbows will hit it as you walk. Custom fitting is not absolutely necessary in all cases. All dimensions given for packs are for average size people and can be scaled up or down as necessary.

The arrangement of the straps that bear on the body is the crucial part of the fit and therefore should be made to measure. The main points to determine placement of these bearing straps are as follows:

1. Lower shoulder strap attachment is near the bottom of the pack.
2. Bottom of the back-band or panel that will support the load against the back should rest slightly below the beltline on the slope of the buttocks. This can vary in position and the most comfortable position should be determined by experiment. Experimenting might consist of trying on an old pack and noting carefully whether it is comfortable, where it rests, etc. Borrowing various packs to check them for comfortable and uncomfortable features is a good way to settle on design. This kind of experimentation will pay off when construction of a pack begins or when design modifications are wanted.
3. Placement of the upper shoulder straps should next be determined. For light loads the pack can be hung from the shoulders, but to attach the straps too low on the back will make it unstable and it will sway from side to side. As the load gets heavier, it will be more comfortable to attach the shoulder straps higher than the shoulders. This requires a frame and creates a wedging action, forcing the pack against the back and eliminating the possibility of its pulling you backward. Compromises will be made and no pack will be perfect for all conditions but the chances are that a little thought given to these considerations will result in a pack superior to most manufactured products.
4. The upper shoulder straps should be placed close enough together to pass over the shoulders close to the neck. If they are attached far apart on the sack they will pass over the shoulders too far from the neck and exert a good deal of uncomfortable leverage. (See Fig. 3, Plate II, p. 52.)

The standard fabric for packs in years past has been a good grade of 10 to 12 ounce double filled army duck. This is a very strong, abrasion resistant, and very water repellent fabric by virtue of its tight weave.

Though a good cotton duck makes a fine pack, where light weight is important the same strength and durability can be obtained from about a 6 ounce nylon, and for a super light pack it is possible to go down to a 3 or 4 ounce nylon. However, there is the old problem of waterproofing nylon which was discussed in the materials section. Nylon cannot be as closely woven as cotton duck. Because of this fact and nylon's filament peculiarities nylon pack fabric should have a plastic coating inside.

Regardless of which fabric is used for packs, except in the very lightest designs, the pack bottoms should be reinforced. This is the part of the pack which will wear out long before the rest of the pack. This reinforcing should cover not only the bottom itself but about 1½″ of the sides and sometimes the bottoms of any side pockets. (Side pocket bottoms should be reinforced when they are low enough to come into contact with the ground when the pack is set down.) Double or triple fabric layers make good reinforcing as does a good grade of chrome tanned garment leather (goatskin, calfskin, pigskin, or capeskin). Leather reinforcing should always be sewn over the fabric before the pack is assembled and never used in place of the fabric. In this way the fabric itself takes the strain of the load and the leather resists the abrasion. (See Figs. 3 and 4, Plate III, p. 55.)

For the very best packs the hardware should be of a solid non-rusting material. Aluminum and stainless steel are rare. The most commonly available material is nickel plated brass. Stay away from painted (japanned) steel; it will nick and rust. Good cadmium plate works well for parts that don't get rubbed too much but will eventually rub off and allow rust. Buckles and snap hooks from army equipment are usually brass under the black oxide finish. Buckles that need adjustment only rarely, such as on shoulder straps, should be of a type that stays put under a load. Buckles on flaps and pockets should be of a type easily operated even with mittens, particularly if the pack is to be used in winter or at high altitudes.

The choice of leather or webbing for straps depends upon personal preference and availability. Occasionally an excellent grade of wide firm nylon webbing is available in surplus stores which can be tapered for attaching buckles. This webbing makes very fine shoulder straps.

A heavy hard leather can be padded with a piece of thick spongy chrome tanned leather. The spongy leather is cut ¾″ wider than the strap, to prevent the strap edges cutting into the shoulders under load. This construction is difficult for the amateur at home. A shoemaker can do the job. He should use nylon thread since the straps are subject to abrasion. The two pieces can be glued as well as sewn for extra strength.

PLATE III

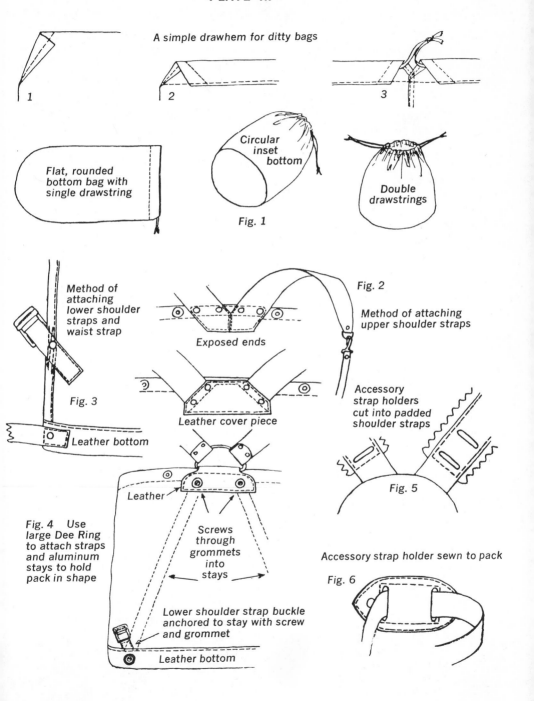

A simple drawhem for ditty bags

1

2

3

Flat, rounded bottom bag with single drawstring

Circular inset bottom

Double drawstrings

Fig. 1

Method of attaching lower shoulder straps and waist strap

Fig. 2

Method of attaching upper shoulder straps

Exposed ends

Fig. 3

Leather bottom

Leather cover piece

Accessory strap holders cut into padded shoulder straps

Fig. 5

Leather

Fig. 4 Use large Dee Ring to attach straps and aluminum stays to hold pack in shape

Screws through grommets into stays

Accessory strap holder sewn to pack

Fig. 6

Lower shoulder strap buckle anchored to stay with screw and grommet

Leather bottom

The zippers used in packs will almost always be subject to hard wear and are difficult to replace when worn out. For this reason die cast, size 5 Coats & Clark Wingsweep zippers or a top grade nylon zipper should be used if at all possible. Care should be taken during the designing of the pack that no zipper is installed in such a way as to have any load applied *across* the closed zipper teeth. This is not because the zipper is apt to pull apart as cheap zippers on luggage will sometimes do—a size 5 Coats & Clark zipper is good for over 90 pounds per inch across the teeth—it is the fact that any zipper mounted across a line of stress is very difficult to close. Also its teeth may be damaged in the process. It is poor practice to install a zipper with a locking slider in such a manner that a load can be applied to it when it is open or partly open. This puts the entire load on the few teeth engaged by the slider and may damage them.

As a good beginning project in the pack department the handy little belt pocket will give practice in handling both instructions and materials. The stiffening band across the back makes it a bit better than the usual similar item available commercially. It makes a fine gadget bag for photographers. Score one in favor of making one's own equipment!

Another good practice project is the ditty bag. These may be used for foods, cases for tents or sleeping bags, cases for blackened cooking pots, or just departmentalizing personal knick-knacks. They can be very simple with a single drawstring top and rounded corners on the bottom. They can also be more elaborate with double drawstring top and inset bottom. (See Fig. 1, Plate III, p. 55.)

DAY PACKS

For the light loads carried on one day trips, bicycle riding, or as a school bag, a frameless sack can be quite comfortable and light. Though the load is not heavy enough to warrant a frame, it is still a convenience and comfort if the pack is not allowed to lose its shape. About the only way to do this is by dividing the interior into several compartments. Partitions for the compartments prevent the gear from falling together in a heap in the bottom of the pack. They also make the pack convenient to use. Even a simple top and bottom division with conventional drawstring around the top and a zippered opening for access to the bottom is a great convenience and an improvement over a simple sack.

Plate III, p. 55, shows some features which may be helpful in designing small frameless packs. Fig. 4 is a design halfway between a frameless pack and a frame rucksack. This has two long pockets from the peak where the shoulder straps are attached at the top down to the lower corners where the straps are attached at the bottom. Into these narrow pockets are inserted curved aluminum strips about $\frac{1}{8}''$ x $\frac{5}{8}''$ or $\frac{3}{4}''$. These hold the pack away from the back and help it hold its shape.

WEEKENDER PACKS

The next larger size pack is the "weekender." Specifically, this pack must be large enough to carry a sleeping bag, a little food, and possibly a tent. This, like the day pack, can be frameless, although in order to have enough room inside for a sleeping bag it is usually impossible to use any inside partitions to help hold the pack in shape. As we have said before the rucksack is fine for weekending. A weekend's supply of equipment can generally be kept well below the weight limit of this type of pack. Its comfort and convenience make it ideal for a pleasant weekend of hiking and climbing.

A removable frame on a rucksack has an advantage. It can be loaded to the limit with the frame in place for backpacking into camp, and then used only partially loaded without frame for a comfortable day's hiking on short trips away from the base.

As a general rule it is best to consider a pack with the maximum load in mind and use it partially loaded for short trips and hikes, rather than to overload a small pack when a longer trip is planned. Overstuffing a pack makes the shape difficult and uncomfortable. Pockets are a great convenience in separating gear and keeping it where it is wanted.

There are several types of frames that can be made for this rucksack. A solid plastic frame will absolutely prevent the contents of the pack from poking through to the wearer's back. A panel of heavy nylon mesh bridged across the curvature of the frame, riveted at the corners, will bear comfortably against the back, distributing the force over the broadest possible area.

One of the best materials for this frame is fiber glass reinforced plastic of the type featured by many hobby shops for home working. Glass fabric, rather than fiber mat, will make the strongest frame. The frame is constructed by making a sandwich of one triangular piece on each surface, two extra bands about 3'' wide across the bottom, and an extra scrap in the peak between the full-sized pieces. The frame must be made on a mold having a compound curve to fit the back. This can be made of papier-mâché, plaster, or an old automobile fender. Instructions for handling the plastic itself should be obtained from the supplier of the plastic.

There is also available a very tough rubber-like thermoplastic called ABS which will become soft and sink into the shape of a dished mold placed under it at 300°F in an ordinary oven. This plastic at ⅛" thickness is slightly heavier than fiber glass but easier to handle. This material should be cut oversize as it shrinks about ½" per foot during heating. (See Fig. 2, Plate IV, p. 59.)

The simplest frame to make is with ¹⁄₃₂" diameter steel or aluminum rod with straps rather than a mesh panel to keep it away from the back. Details of construction for these are shown in Fig. 3, Plate IV, p. 59.

There are several accessories which can be advantageous with this size weekender pack. Sponge rubber pads for the shoulder straps are wonderful for bony shoulders. These are made very neatly by wrapping a piece of nylon around a piece of sponge rubber. The nylon is wrapped around the rubber and lapped about ½" in over the top side. It is secured to the rubber by stitching through around the edge. Two or three short pieces of webbing across the rubber under which the pack straps slip are included in the stitching. The advantage of this type of construction is that the sticky rubber is left exposed where it is in contact with the shoulder straps thus holding the pads in position, while the side that goes against the shirt is slippery nylon which makes it easy to slip into the pack.

It is very difficult to sew sponge rubber on most sewing machines. Heavy cotton thread must be used with an extra large needle. A ⅜" sponge rubber pad will do the job, but anything up to ¾" is better if it can be sewn. Since these pads are so small, hand sewing will probably be just as easy. (See Fig. 4, Plate IV, p. 59.)

Most packs have drawstrings around the top for closure. In summer these are only a nuisance to tie and untie, but in cold weather it can be downright dangerous to remove a mitten to get into a pack. The same situation exists with clothing and sleeping bag drawstrings. A neat little drawstring clamp can be turned out of plastic or aluminum if a drill press is available. A piece of rod is first drilled almost as deep as it is long. This makes a case into which slides a length of smaller rod (the plunger) with a small compression spring behind it. Before inserting the spring, measure its length when fully compressed. Put a scrap of something in the hole of the case which will prevent the plunger's going in any farther than the fully compressed spring would allow it. Drill a cross hole through the case and plunger. Put the spring back in the case and compress it with the plunger until the cross holes line up. Pull both ends of the drawstring through the cross holes in the same direction. Release the plunger and the drawstrings are held tight, press it and the clamp can be adjusted to any position. (See Fig. 5, Plate IV, p. 59.)

A simple little clamp can be made from a piece of stiff leather or plastic for drawstrings which don't get such rough service, such as clothing drawstrings. Four holes are punched in a square of leather or plastic.

PLATE IV

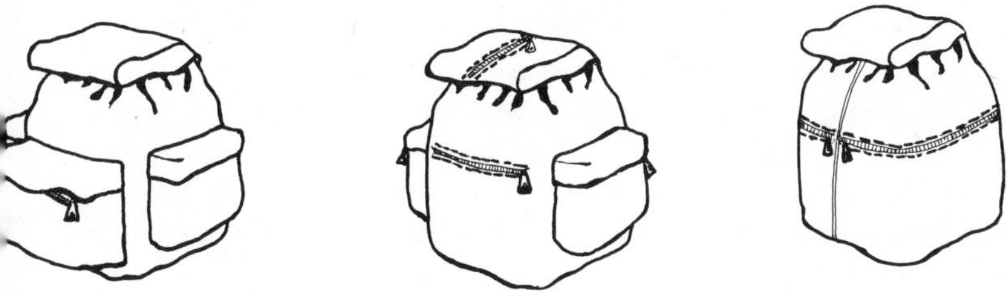

Fig. 1

Pocket arrangements

Fig. 2 Solid Fiberglas frame with mesh panel

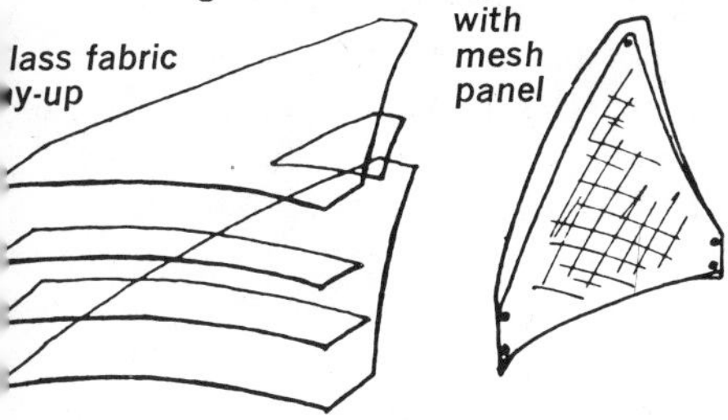

...lass fabric
...y-up

Fig. 3

Two frames of solid rod with webbing support

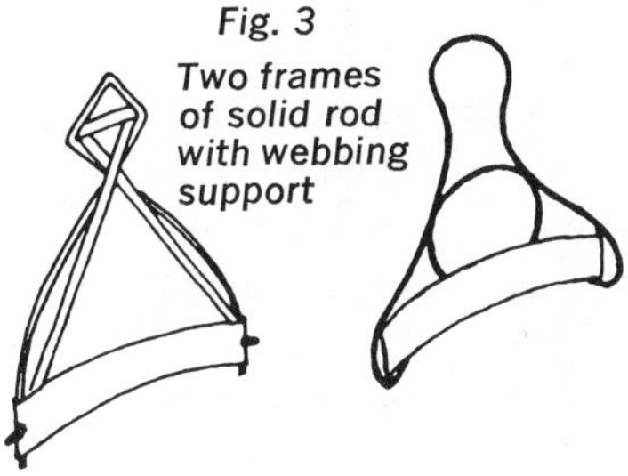

Fig. 4

Shoulder pad

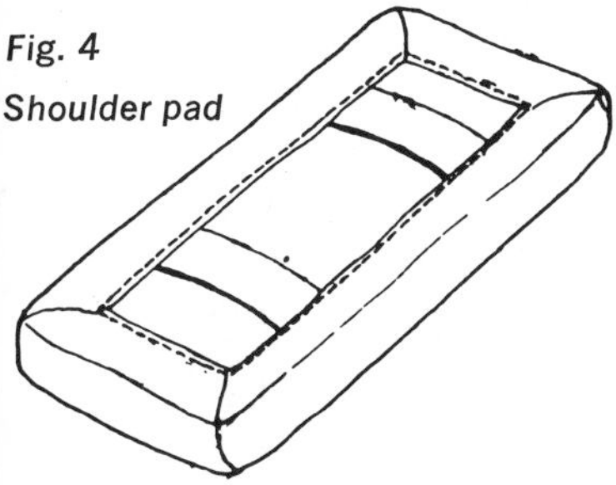

Fig. 5

Drawstring clamp

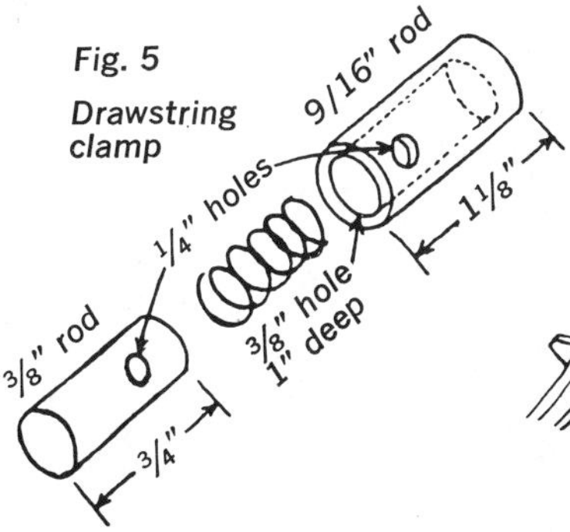

9/16" rod

1/4" holes

3/8" rod

3/8" hole 1" deep

1 1/8"

3/4"

Fig. 6

Leather drawstring clamp

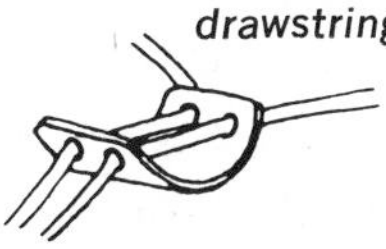

Fig. 7

Friction cord

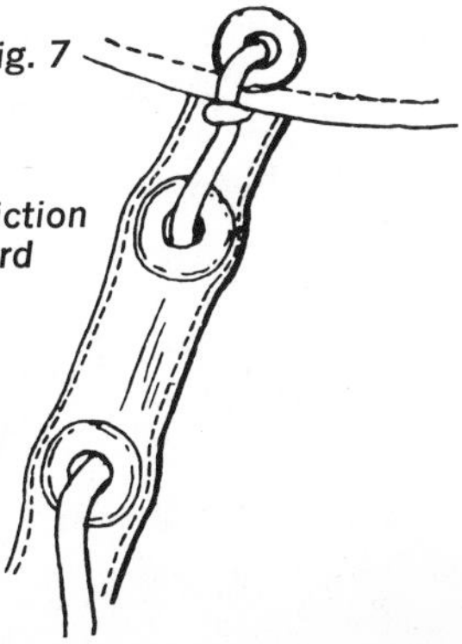

Fig. 8

Ice ax carrier

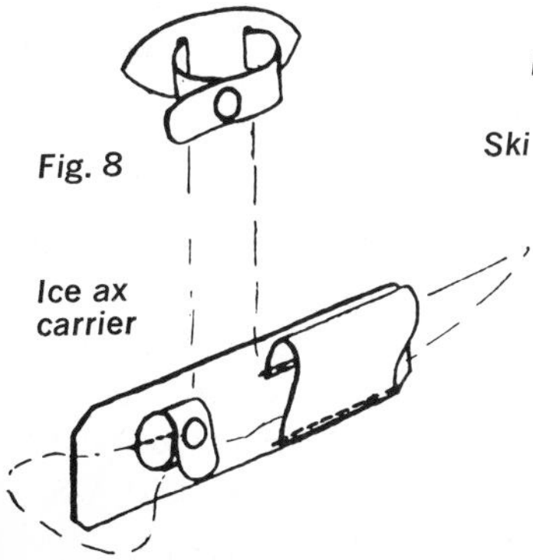

Fig. 9

Ski carrier

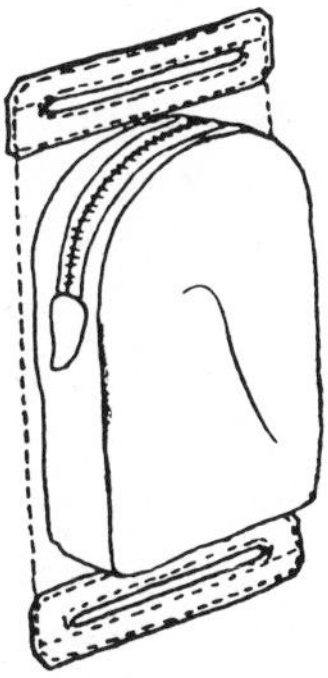

When squeezed into a fold so the holes face each other the clamp slides easily, but when it flattens itself out it grips the cords. (See Fig. 6, Plate IV, p. 59.)

One way to hold pack flaps down without using buckles which are difficult to work with mittens on is to run a cord through two grommets set in a piece of webbing as shown in Fig. 7, Plate IV. The webbing is sewn tightly to the pack and the friction of the cord passing behind it will hold the flap down. The cord should be long enough so the flap can be pulled completely out of the way.

For mountain climbers there is the recurring problem of what to do with the ice ax when it is not being held. It is sometimes stuck head down in the pack, but this can be difficult in the middle of a cliff. A little leather gadget made and attached to the pack allows the ice ax to be snapped in and out at will even in the most difficult spots. A flap is sewn to a rectangular base of leather to take the pick of the ax. A suitable distance behind it a small snap loop of leather is sewn to go around the neck of the adz to hold it in position. This assembly is sewn to the lowest possible position on the back of the pack. As high as possible on the pack a leather holder for an accessory strap is sewn. Through this is inserted a short snap or buckle strap to go around the shaft of the ax. A similar type of carrier can be designed to hold tripods, fishing poles, or other ungainly but frequently needed items. (See Fig. 8, Plate IV, p. 59.)

PACK BOARDS

In the domain of the pack board will be included all the sacks, even though some of them are only of weekend capacity, that use a pack board type of frame for their foundation. The sacks themselves are constructed in the same manner as the rucksacks described before—using the same kinds of outside pockets, leather bottoms, and other features. The major difference is that the patterns for these packs are generally easier to lay out because they are essentially rectangular. Since the straps are not attached to the sack itself, the top edge and flap treatments are different.

Most sacks are removable from the pack boards so the boards themselves may be used alone to carry miscellaneous loads. The method by which the sack is attached to the frame is important. The most generally satisfactory way is to use two long tabs in the side seams of the sack that are attached at intervals to the frame. Some use studs attached to the frame with grommets in the tabs. Some use loose pins through the grommets and held by a wire, but loose parts always increase the possibility of loss. From an engineering standpoint it would probably be better to support the load from the top edge of the sack than from the sides, so if the pack board itself has a bar or edge across the top, the sack can be attached along this and then held at the sides only to prevent shifting from side to side. A leather or fabric flap should be sewn to the sack and folded over the top edge of the board and then fastened. This distributes the strain much better than just fastening sack to board along the top edge.

Some sacks hang on the horns of the pack board with little pockets. This is satisfactory for light loads but you can see the small area over which maybe 40 pounds per pocket must be absorbed by the fabrics of the sack. It is a potential point of failure.

The important thing to remember about transferring strain, which usually is applied at a point, is to spread it out. For example if a load of 100 pounds is to be attached via a piece of 1″ web to a fabric having a tensile strength of only 50 pounds per inch, the fabric would rip if the web were sewn directly to it. You must double the fabric with a reinforcing piece to make it equal to the strain at the point of attachment and then spread the reinforcement out to a 2″ width before sewing it to the original fabric. This spreads the 100-pound strain over 2″, or 50 pounds per inch which the fabric can take.

It is often a great advantage to have a relatively small sack for the pack board, and yet have provision for the expansion of the sack to full size when it is needed. One way to do this is to attach the sack somewhere short of the top edge of the board. By using an inside sleeve around the top of the pack, the sack can be pulled out and extended when needed and tucked down inside when the small sack is needed. The top of the sleeve has grommets and a drawstring just like the top of the sack. (See Fig. 3, Plate V, p. 62.)

It is often useful to have a sack that can be used by itself without the pack board. In this case shoulder straps must be attached to the sack. These separate shoulder straps can be of the design used on a day pack or light rucksack and should usually be attached at the top, just below the arrangement for attachment to the pack board. A 6″ square patch of fabric can be sewn on first for general reinforcing. The straps should then be attached following the same method as that described for the Zephyr Pack, using a leather cover patch over the strap ends with several rivets. The lower straps should be attached at a seam or point that offers a little reinforcement to spread the strain. If this is impossible, some extra fabric patches should be sewn on here for reinforcing.

Since most pack board sacks are cut to fit a rectangular board they are not going to be quite as comfortable as a rucksack when used by themselves with their own straps. However, they can be made to double very nicely as a one-day pack provided they are never overloaded.

PLATE V

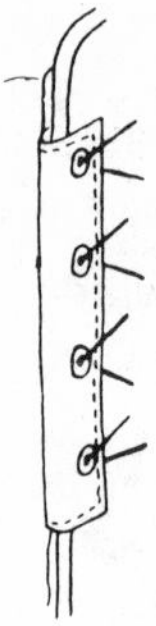

Fig. 2

Grommet flap to hold sides of sack

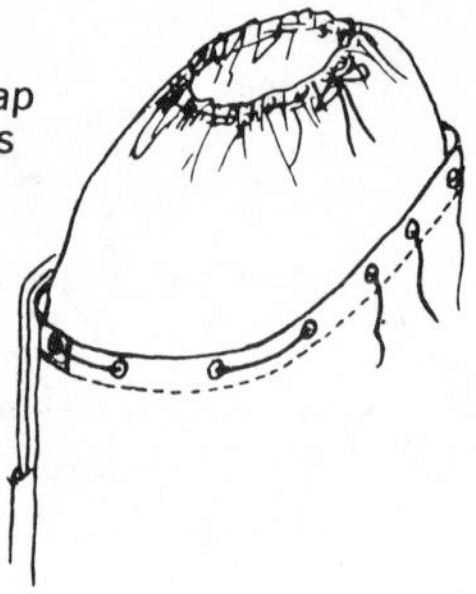

Fig. 3

Extension sleeve on sack

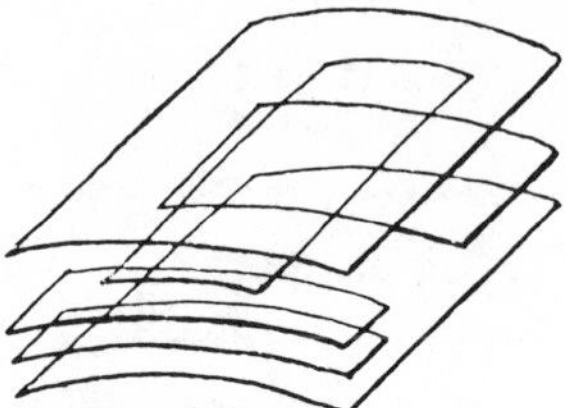

Glass fabric lay-up

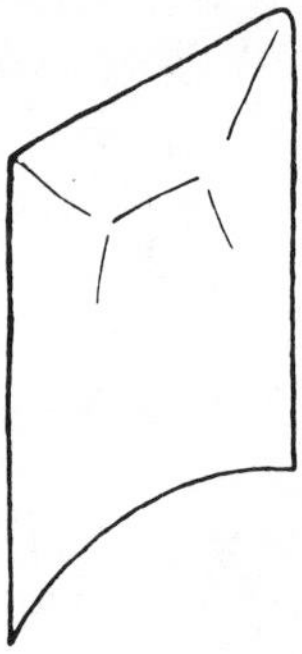

Fig. 4

Fiberglas pack board

Fig. 5   Plywood and birch dowels

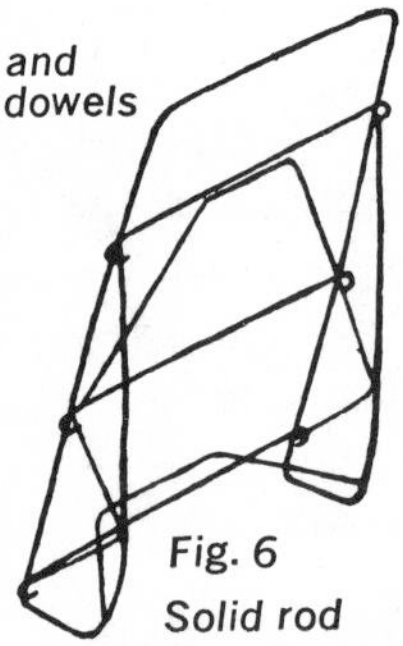

Fig. 6   Solid rod

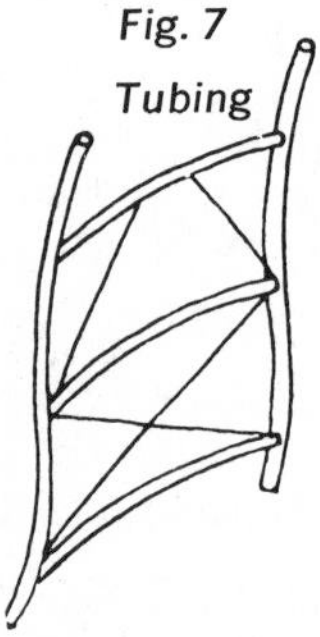

Fig. 7   Tubing

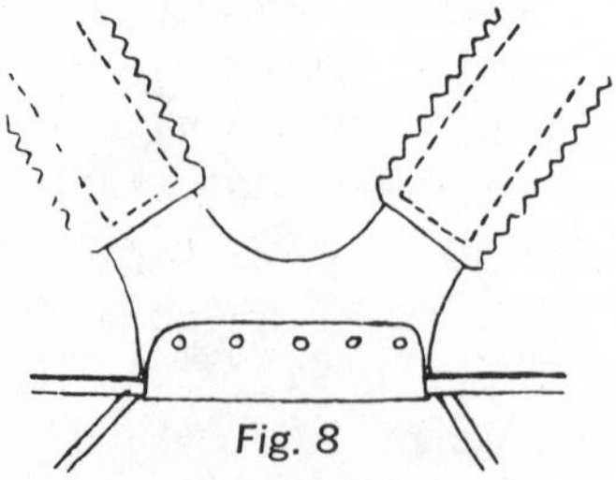

Fig. 8

Leather shoulder yoke

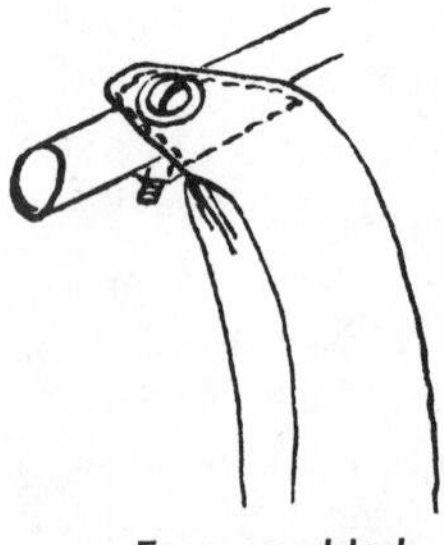

Foam padded shoulder straps

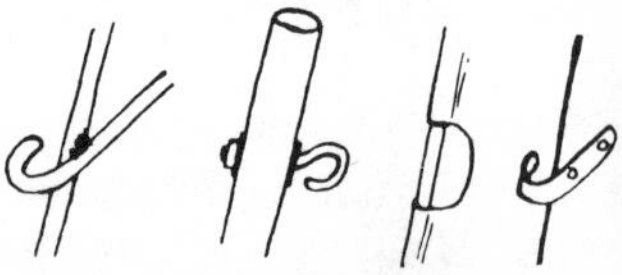

Fig. 10   Lashing hooks

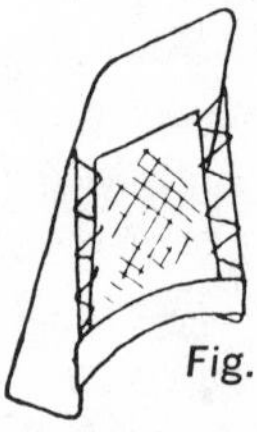

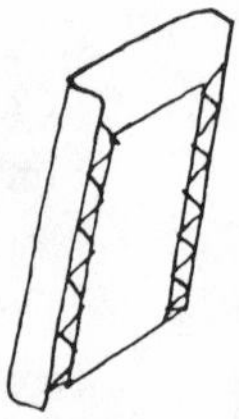

Fig. 11

Curved panel   Tight panel

The pack boards themselves can be of more varied design than the sacks. They can be made of wood, plastic, sheet aluminum, aluminum or steel rod, aluminum or magnesium tubing. They can be anything from a simple frame which holds the sack in shape to a large board with lashing hooks and a shelf at the bottom for carrying large and heavy loads of miscellaneous equipment. The support for the back may be anything from a canvas panel to string lacing. The important points to remember are:

1. The load is going to be supported against the entire back so the board must fit the back comfortably.
2. The board should extend relatively high so the load will be placed over the legs with only a slight forward lean to the body.
3. The lower shoulder straps should be attached as far to the rear of the board as possible so the weight of the load will tend to thrust forward onto the back. The upper shoulder straps should be as broad as possible to distribute the load over as wide an area as possible. (See Fig. 8, Plate V, p. 62.)

Many pack boards, such as the Yukon and the Trapper Nelson, have been made of wood in the past. This is still possibly the simplest material to work with but it won't produce a strong board that is really light. Even the molded plywood board of the army, which is beyond the ability of most amateurs to make, is heavier than need be, though quite durable for army use. Fiber glass reinforced plastic can be used to advantage here. The advantages of fiber glass are its solid surface which prevents any of the load from poking through to the back, and its durability and light weight. Provision for hooks or other fixtures for attaching the lash rope is often a problem that discourages using plastic for a large size pack board. Some type of hook riveted on would be the easiest construction. An edge reinforced with metal rod with the plastic cut back from the rod at intervals, though sturdier, would require that the lash rope be threaded through each time it is used. This arrangement would be much better if the pack board is to be used for tough going through heavy brush where almost any kind of hook tends to catch in every small branch as it brushes past.

Almost all the better commercial pack boards are made of tubing, either aluminum or magnesium. For the slight additional difficulty of fabrication, the magnesium seems well worth the effort to achieve the ultimate in a light weight board. Reynolds aluminum tubing however is now available in most hardware stores. Magnesium is hard to find. Both aluminum and magnesium are difficult to weld and not every welding shop can do a good job. A good idea is to let the prospective welder do a few sample Tee joints, then try to break them apart with a hammer to see if he did a satisfactory job. Undoubtedly a good man with a Heli-Arc outfit can do the highest quality welds on these metals. If a good riveted design can be worked out it will eliminate the soft annealed spots in the frame that result from the welding.

The lightest weight board is one of simple ladder design with curved rungs and side pieces, either straight or with an S curve to fit the back, made of ½″ magnesium tubing. Some sort of bracing must be provided for the cross piece that carries the upper shoulder strap attachment, except on boards designed for the lightest loads. This bracing can be expanded to help close up the wide open spaces left between the cross pieces. The need for closing up these spaces is greatest at the bottom of the frame and least, near the top.

There is no doubt that tubing will make the lightest, most rigid pack board, but it does have disadvantages. If a disaster befalls the pack, such as a fall over a cliff, or a pack animal losing its load, in which the frame becomes bent it is usually impossible to straighten it. Tubing of thin wall section will cave in when bent very far and will break when straightened.

Solid rod, if it is properly welded, will make a board that can be bent into a pretzel and still be pounded back into shape. This feature is well worth considering for heavy expedition work. By using a solid rod having a spring temper it is possible to design a flexible frame that will take a lot of abuse without permanent damage. The use of rod is also very convenient in some minor details such as forming lashing hooks as an integral part of the frame. Rod also lends itself well to the design of a frame with a flat cargo surface with plenty of depth at the bottom. The flat cargo surface is much more convenient than most other arrangements for attaching loads. Because of these features, the solid rod construction is recommended for heavy expedition pack boards. However, it is recognized that with pains and skill a superior board may often be custom made out of other materials.

Aluminum rod can be used for this type of construction but it must be remembered that welding will anneal the rod and the smaller diameter of the rod as compared to tubing will allow it to bend much more easily in these places. A spring tempered steel rod of $\frac{7}{32}$″ diameter will weigh little more than good rugged aluminum tubing. Cold drawn 18-8 stainless steel rod is ideal in all respects, although ordinary cold rolled steel rod will do.

Steel will be annealed in the welding but its greater inherent strength will eliminate the bending if care is taken in the design and no welds are put in the middle of the cross pieces. In the sketch of the suggested design for this type of board there are no welds where the brace carrying the shoulder straps run parallel to the cross piece, nor where the bottom curved brace and shelf extension cross over the cross piece. The only welds are on the sides. Note also the ease with which the lashing hooks are formed on the ends of the cross pieces. They are curved until the ends are actually inside the frame to avoid catching branches. Most pack boards can use a narrow shelf across the bottom. This keeps the load from slipping down under constant bouncing.

The depth at the bottom of the frame is a very important comfort consideration with very heavy loads. Most of the boards discussed previously will have to depend on a panel, or band laced across the curvature of the frame to support the load on the back. This means that the contact with the back is limited to the curvature formed by the push of the load against the tightly laced panel or band. With a deep frame, one that comes halfway around the body, it is possible to use a curved band, as on a rucksack frame, that contacts the entire curve of the back from side to side. This distributes the load over a much wider area and gives the board greater stability due to its body-hugging features. (See Fig. 11, Plate V, p. 62.) This also accommodates a load carrying waist strap better.

Unfortunately, however, if the lower shoulder straps are attached to these forward corners of the deep frames, as is so often the case, the shift in this critical pivot point will tend to make the pack fall away from the back thus defeating the advantage of the pack board. If the frame has depth at the bottom to allow a comfortably curved support band, then it must have some point well to the rear for attaching the lower straps.

It should be pointed out here that a board which curves over the head allowing the load to be placed high and forward over the legs is very good for trails and general hiking. For mountain climbing, however, as we have said, it is often necessary to look up to see the route and bumping the head on this forward portion of the pack board can become a nuisance. Its high center of gravity is a disadvantage on rough terrain.

For the ultimate in comfort a pack board should be made to fit the body of the person using it. It should be wide enough to reach around the hips but not so wide that the elbows hit it. Its height should be as great as consistent with the use to which it will be put. Remember to secure a place for attaching the upper shoulder straps as determined by the method described at the beginning of the chapter. The depth at the bottom should be about 4".

The actual attachment of straps to the pack board merits careful consideration. The lower straps can be ¾" webbing or leather. They should attach as far to the rear as possible so the load will be tipped against the back. This rearward attachment sometimes makes it difficult to slip into the pack. This problem can be solved by inserting a snap hook and dee ring arrangement to allow the straps to be opened while the pack is slipped on.

In the case of the solid rod frame suggested, the straps may be riveted loosely around the bottom rod so they can be slipped forward for getting into the harness and then slipped to the rear corners after the board is on the back.

Since the pack board is designed to carry maximum weight the best and firmest leather or web should be used for the upper shoulder straps—at least 2½″ wide. A wide padded strap similar to those used on the smaller packs but with more padded area can be used. It is possible to fasten the straps directly to the frame but it is more comfortable if a leather yoke, cut to fit close to the neck and over the shoulders, is used to locate the straps definitely on the body as illustrated by Fig. 8, Plate V, p. 62. If the straps are attached separately to the frame they should be held close to one another where they leave the frame so they pass close on either side of the neck. If they bear too far out on the shoulders the leverage exerted will be very tiring on neck and shoulder muscles.

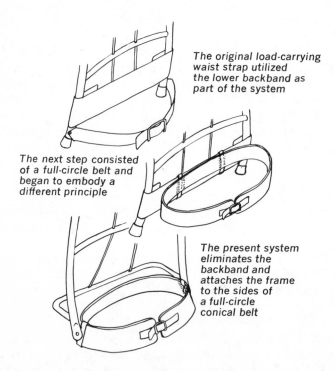

The original load-carrying waist strap utilized the lower backband as part of the system

The next step consisted of a full-circle belt and began to embody a different principle

The present system eliminates the backband and attaches the frame to the sides of a full-circle conical belt

Last we come to the method of supporting the frame and load against the back. The simplest method is to use a canvas panel, the full size of the frame up to the shoulder straps, wrapped around the frame and laced together at the back. This helps to close the open areas of the frame and is the usual method used with wood pack boards. As mentioned before, this panel is hot and heavy. A panel of heavy nylon mesh laced to the sides of a tubular or solid rod frame is relatively cool and saves considerable weight. This nylon mesh panel is sewn to the leather band at the bottom of the board.

The heaviest part of the bearing weight comes at the bottom of the board. A heavy leather, or other firm material, band at least 3" wide is a good idea at this point. This should be adjustable by passing the leather around the edges of the frame and lacing it together behind. The lightest frames can use another similar but lighter band about halfway up the frame. The two bands are also cool but may not give great enough distribution of weight to be comfortable under heavy loads.

One excellent method of supporting the frame that is traditionally applied to Trapper Nelson boards by knowing users is the string lacing. This consists of light cord laced back and forth through holes drilled about 1" apart along the edges of the board. This gives light weight and very cool support, but is not good for the heaviest loads.

The subject of packs is almost inexhaustible. Their design can be as personal as a well tailored suit. With thought and care put into the design the pack will reward its owner many times over. His back will really know the difference!

There is one heavy load pack accessory commonly used, which can give a good deal of added comfort. This is the waist strap. This is a wide strap attached low on the board so it can support the load. The idea is to hunch your shoulders to raise the load. Then cinch up on your waist strap. When you relax you will find most of the load now on your hips.

Belt Pocket

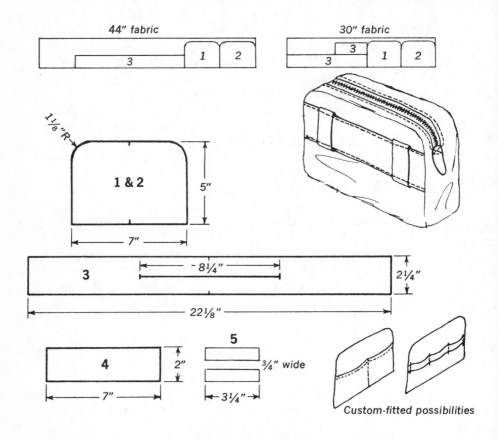

44" fabric

30" fabric

1⅛"R

1 & 2

5"

7"

3

- 8¼" -

2¼"

22⅛"

4

2"

7"

5

¾" wide

3¼"

Custom-fitted possibilities

BELT POCKET

An Easy Beginning Project

LIST OF MATERIALS
Fabric—6" of 44" or 30" wide
2" Web—7"; or 7" x 2" piece of heavy leather
¾" Web—11½"; or 8½" of ¾" leather
Zipper—one 8" pocket style, or open top

INSTRUCTIONS

1. Read "Patterns and Sewing" to familiarize yourself with operations and terms used.
2. Lay out and cut parts, piecing no. 3 Gusset if necessary as indicated for 30″ fabric. Allow ⅜″ extra on each piece for rough flat felled piecing seam. All other seam allowances are included in the dimensions.
3. Sew zipper into slit in no. 3 Gusset with leather or web pull tabs at the ends.
4. Cut parts no. 4 and no. 5 of web or leather.
5. Place parts no. 5 across part no. 4 about 1¼″ in from each end. Tuck ends around edge of no. 4 and stitch close to edge to hold in position.
6. Sew assembly as prepared in step 5 across the top of no. 2 Back, ¾″ down from edge.
7. If you want to add any inside pockets or loops of elastic to hold specific camera accessories or first aid supplies, etc., now is the time to do it. Sew them to the insides of no. 1 Front or no. 2 Back.
8. Starting at the bottom center marks, sew edge of no. 3 Gusset around edge of no. 2 Back with a plain seam ¼″ in from edge. Use seam binding tape if desired. Repeat with other edge around no. 1 Front and turn right side out.

Echo Pack

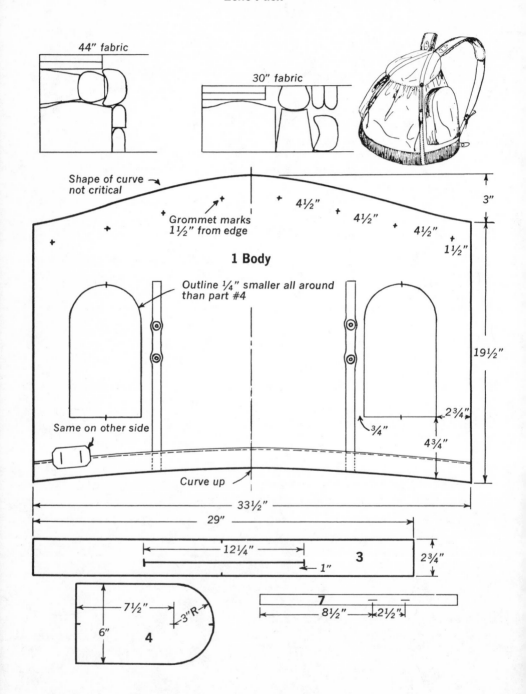

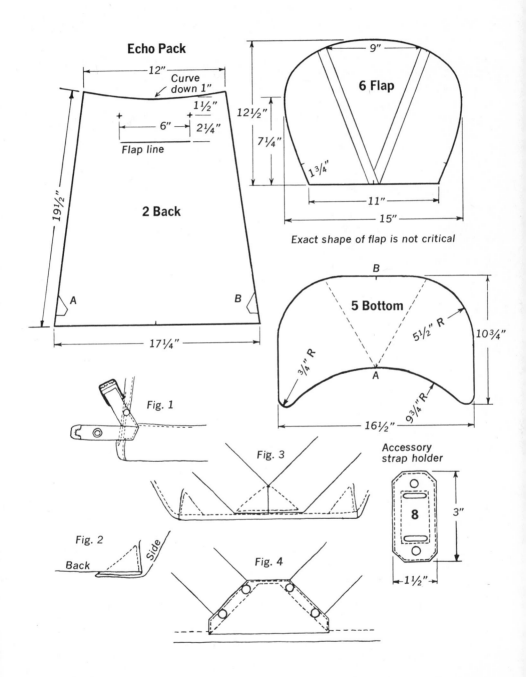

Echo Pack

12"
Curve down 1"
1½"
6"
2¼"
Flap line

2 Back

19½"

A   B

17¼"

9"

6 Flap

12½"
7¼"
1¾"
11"
15"

Exact shape of flap is not critical

B
5 Bottom
5½" R
10¾"
¾" R
A
9¾" R
16½"

Fig. 1

Fig. 3

Fig. 2

Back

Side

Fig. 4

Accessory strap holder

8

3"

1½"

ECHO PACK

LIST OF MATERIALS

Fabric—41″ of 44″ wide or 62″ of 30″ wide

¾″ Webbing—9 feet, or ¾″ leather strap—9 feet

Nylon cord—8 feet

1½″ Webbing—3 feet, or 2″ leather strap—3 feet

Heavy leather—5″ x 7″ for strap end cover piece and 4 accessory strap holders

Soft leather—16″ x 17″ for leather bottom, or this may be of same fabric as pack, in which case increase fabric by 1 foot. Double bottom is optional but advised.

Buckles—2, for ¾″ strap

Snap hooks—2, optional for use in shoulder straps, ¾″

Dee rings—2, optional for use in shoulder straps, ¾″

Strap tips—4, for ¾″ strap

Grommets—18, size no. 1

Zippers—2, 12″ long, pocket style or open top

INSTRUCTIONS

1. Read "Patterns and Sewing" to familiarize yourself with the terms and operations used.
2. Lay out and cut parts. Be sure to include 2 each of parts no. 3 and no. 4. Cut second part no. 5 Bottom either of fabric or soft leather and enough of the same material 1½″ wide to run across the bottom edge of part no. 1 Body. Mark position for pockets, etc., on right side of fabric.
3. Sew zippers into slits on parts no. 3 Gussets with leather or web pull tabs at the ends if desired.
4. Join ends of parts no. 3 with a plain seam to form a loop. Then, starting with this seam at the bottom center mark of part no. 4 Pocket, sew the edge of part no. 3 that is farthest from the zipper, around the edge of part no. 4. Use a plain seam with seam binding tape if desired and adjust parts as necessary so top center marks coincide.
5. Sew the pockets to part no. 1 Body at location marked. Use a top stitch seam. Start with bottom center key mark and seam in Gusset no. 3 even and adjust so top center marks also coincide.
6. Cut two 15″ lengths of ¾″ web or leather. Cut slits ½″ long for grommets as indicated on part no. 7 and set grommets. Sew these to part no. 1 alongside pockets as indicated. Start with end B at bottom of part no. 1 and sew up one edge and down the other. Turn top under if web is used. Be careful when sewing around the grommets. It may

be necessary to hold the material down with a screwdriver when the machine presser foot is up on the grommet to make it stitch.

7. Sew 1½″ wide strip of leather or fabric, whichever is being used for bottom, across bottom edge of part no. 1 Body, as indicated.

8. Cut two Accessory Strap Holders, part no. 8, from the heavy leather and sew below and forward of each side pocket as indicated.

9. Sew edges of part no. 2 Back to edges of part no. 1 Body with a flat felled seam; finished felled seam if fabric is light enough.

10. If no snap hooks are used in the shoulder straps, cut 2 pieces of ¾″ web or leather 15″ long. Tip both ends if web is used. Sew to outside of part no. 2 at locations A and B. See detail Fig. 1, except that instead of a buckle, the upper end is 12″ long, and will attach to the buckle of the upper shoulder strap. If snap hooks are used in the shoulder straps, proceed as follows: cut 2 6″ lengths of ¾″ web or leather. Tip one end if webbing is used. Sew onto outside of part no. 2 at locations A and B including a buckle. See detail drawing Fig. 1. The extended tab is to be used in attaching the sack to a frame and will be fitted with whatever hardware is needed later. These tabs will accommodate a frame 18″ wide. If a different size is needed this is the time to adjust the tab length. If no frame is to be used the tabs can be omitted, or they can be used as a waist strap if they are made longer.

11. Hem around the top of the sack with a plain hem that finishes ¾″ wide. Fold this against the inside of the sack. Set grommets as indicated on drawings of parts no. 1 and no. 2.

12. Sew the two parts no. 5 Bottom together with a vee of stitching as indicated.

13. Sew the bottom into the pack with a plain seam. Use binding tape if desired. Start with bottom center mark part no. 2 on mark A part no. 5 and adjust so mark B part no. 5 falls on bottom center mark part no. 1.

14. Sew trim web to part no. 6 Flap on outside as indicated.

15. Box rear corners of Flap at marks as indicated in detail drawing, Fig. 2. Sew a plain hem around edge of flap about ⅜″ wide. Set two grommets in ends of trim web.

16. Sew flap to sack at top of part no. 2 on line marked. Stitch back and forth several times at ends. Center flap on the marked line.

17. Prepare web or leather shoulder straps 1½″ to 2″ wide and 18″ long. Cut taper in leather or sew taper in web. If snap hooks are not used attach buckles. If snap hooks are used attach dee rings to ends. Cut other end to shape approximately as shown in detail drawing Fig. 3. Cut two more accessory strap holders and sew to outside of shoulder straps 2″ from end. Sew onto sack over flap and with edges of straps just above flap hem as in Fig. 3. Center straps between flap corners.

18. Cut cover patch of heavy leather and sew on as shown in Fig. 4. The bottom is left open to receive the top of a frame if one is to be used, otherwise it can be sewn closed too.

19. Omit this step if snap hooks and dee rings are not used in the shoulder straps. Cut two lengths of ¾" web or leather 12" long. If web, set tips in one end. Rivet a snap hook on the other end and attach to lower shoulder buckles. Snap hook into upper shoulder dee rings.

20. Set rivets as follows:
    4 in shoulder straps as in Fig. 4
    8 in accessory strap holders as in Part no. 8 drawing
    2 in lower shoulder straps as in Fig. 1

21. Cut two pieces of nylon cord 24" long and one 48" long. Thread the 48" piece around top grommets for a draw cord and knot the ends. Tie the ends of the 24" cords to the flap grommets and thread the other ends in the top friction grommet and out the lower one. A large crochet hook no. 00 is good for this. Knot the ends to keep the cords from pulling back through the friction grommets. This will provide enough friction to hold the flap closed yet it can be opened by simply pulling it back.

CHAPTER V SLEEPING BAGS

Conserving the body's warmth is the main purpose of the sleeping bag. The physical comfort, a soft place to sleep, is secondary and is usually supplied by some means other than the bag.

There is wide latitude in what constitutes an acceptable sleeping bag for use in summer when not much heat loss need be expected. For winter and extreme cold this is less true. Then use must be made of every factor in design and materials that contributes to the insulating properties of the bag. If this is not done, the outfit resulting from careless design will be too heavy and bulky to be practical, or too cold to be comfortable.

Sometimes features of convenience are not compatible with warmth but can be made use of in a summer bag. The summer bag can be rectangular and roomy. It can be made with a zipper down one side and across the bottom allowing the bag to open out into a nice quilt for use at home or on cabin beds. This same zipper, if it is of the separating type, can be used with a similar bag to join two single bags into one large one. The top end of the bag may be left completely open for freedom of movement. The tubes holding the insulation can be made by stitching the inside fabric directly to the outside fabric. Each of these is a feature of convenience but detrimental to the overall insulation of a bag to be used at low temperatures. For very low temperatures only bags filled with down with gusseted or diaphragmed compartments, running around the bag rather than lengthwise, will be considered.

A bag suitable for below zero temperatures should be formfitting, tapering at the foot end and fitting closely around the body. Heat loss is proportional to the surface area; the smaller the area of the bag the less the heat loss from that source.

SHELL CONSTRUCTION

Zippers are a great convenience, but they are a fine place to lose heat and they are likely to snag. Large size zippers may not snag less, but there is generally more clearance between the slider and the teeth so if it does snag the fabric you can pull it free again without tearing. To keep weight down, zippers should be molded or coil nylon which weighs less than metal.

As for heat loss, most manufacturers back up the zipper with a down filled tube that is supposed to plug the gap. This is usually faced with a piece of tape or web to reduce the tendency to catch in the slider. A better way is to use two zippers. One closes the outer shell and the other closes the lining. When complete protection is needed both zippers are closed and the thickness of the bag is maintained. A zipper backed by a flap held closed with Velcro tape is also draft proof.

On full length zippers that run down one full side and across the foot, it is important to use plastic zippers from a weight standpoint. The difference between nylon and metal in size 5 is about a quarter pound. With the advent of the nylon separating double zipper, which opens from either end, it is possible to have zip-together bags now that allow ventilation at the foot end. For maximum efficiency in a winter bag, no zipper at all is used.

For extremely cold temperatures, two single bags that zip together to make a double bag increase the surface area and thus the heat loss beyond what is necessary. The more efficient solution is to make the double bag the actual dimensions of the two people who are to use it. If it is made as snug as is comfortable for two people lying flat on their backs with arms at sides the bag will be less than two-thirds the size of two single bags. It will give a surprising amount of room for various other sleeping positions. If the bag is for very cold weather use, it should fit close and snug around the head to avoid heat loss around the neck. Two methods of doing this are illustrated in Fig. 2, Plate VI, p. 77.

Other design refinements are necessary as the temperature goes down. Condensed moisture from the breath inside the bag can ruin half its insulating value in a couple of nights. Obviously then it is a good idea to draw the bag close about the neck so that the breath does not go down inside the bag. The head and face protection are thus separate from the body functionally, though not actually detached. This can be done effectively by having a drawstring, preferably with an elastic section in it, just above the shoulders. With this arrangement it is possible to have just a square top bag and detachable hood if desired.

Because of the moisture condensation it should also be pointed out that no sleeping bag should be made with a plastic coated outer fabric. The human body gives up about one pint of moisture during a night and it is essential that this moisture be given an avenue of escape. If the outer layer of the bag is impermeable and its temperature is below the condensation point all this moisture will condense on its inside surface and soak back into the insulation, eventually destroying its value. Some special part of a regular bag, such as the bottom, can be made with an impermeable outer

PLATE VI

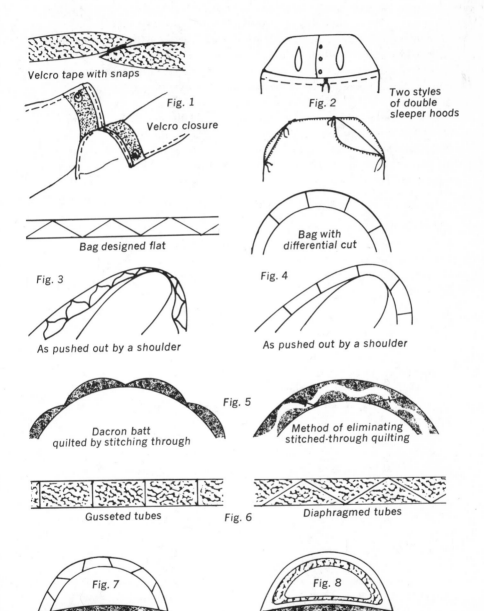

Velcro tape with snaps

Velcro closure

Fig. 1

Two styles of double sleeper hoods

Fig. 2

Bag designed flat

Bag with differential cut

Fig. 3

As pushed out by a shoulder

Fig. 4

As pushed out by a shoulder

Fig. 5

Dacron batt quilted by stitching through

Method of eliminating stitched-through quilting

Gusseted tubes

Fig. 6

Diaphragmed tubes

Fig. 7

Section of Mountain Sleeper showing padded bottom

Fig. 8

Section of Arctic Sleeper Shell with an all down filled bag inside layer, provided a similar impermeable layer is used on the inside surface to prevent the body's moisture ever reaching the cold outer layer. This allows the inside surface to warm up above the condensation point. In effect this encases the insulation between two water vapor proof layers and keeps it dry and efficient under all conditions. Even with a bag that breathes it is essential to ventilate adequately in use and dry it out frequently because if the bag is insulating properly the outer layer will often be below the dew point and will therefore condense part of the moisture passing through it so that the bag will gradually become damp.

The lining of such a close fitting bag, especially if there is no zipper, should be of a slippery fabric—nylon is the lightest and toughest—making it easy to slip into. True, nylon feels chilly at first, but its ability to soak heat from the body is less than cotton flannel for instance so it warms quickly.

INSULATION

The biggest contributory factor to the warmth of a sleeping bag is the amount of insulation it gives. Insulation must be had against conductive and convective heat loss for the most part. Radiant heat loss is a very small part of the total.

Conductive heat loss through the top of the bag is kept at an inconsequential level by any material of low enough density to act as an effective convective insulator.

Convective heat loss refers to the transfer of heat through the movement of the surrounding air. This heat transfer can be caused by the wind, and by stirring up of the air mechanically such as by the bellows action in the bag when the person turns and tosses, or by setting up of currents due to temperature differences.

Air is the medium of convective heat loss, but is also one of the best insulators so that if the possibility of forming convection currents can be eliminated, it becomes the ideal insulation. There is considerable drag on the air adjacent to any smooth surface. Within $\frac{1}{8}''$ of a smooth surface this drag almost prevents the movement of the air. Outward from this point the air is free to move more and more. By breaking up the air into pockets measuring less than $\frac{1}{4}''$ across its ability to carry heat away by convection can be eliminated.

For the reasons discussed in the Insulation section of "Materials," the greater the thickness of immobilized air the greater the insulation provided. It is the thickness, and only the thickness, that determines the amount of insulation. Whether it is down, kapok, or steelwool that is used to immobilize the air makes very little difference in the actual value of insulation. There are no miracle materials that give more insulation per inch of thickness. Thus the selection of an insulating material for the top of a sleeping bag depends on several things. First, it should be the lightest weight possible to fill a given thickness and provide this area with dead air. Second, it should compress into the smallest possible space for packing. Third, it should spring back to its original thickness when unpacked; and fourth, it must perform this cycle many times without wearing out. To fill these conditions nothing better than good waterfowl down has been found to date. A 50-50 mixture of good quality feathers and down filling the same thickness will be slightly heavier and will not compress quite as much. Dacron batting will be even a little heavier and compress a little less.

Insulating material for the bottom of the bag, the part one lies on, must have different characteristics. It too should be of the lightest possible weight which will provide the necessary thickess of insulation. However, if this portion of the insulation is as easily compressible as the top of the bag, it will be compressed by the weight of the body and thus lose its thickness—i.e., its insulating value. Therefore, insulation for the bottom of the bag should resist compression as much as possible.

There are various materials which meet these two requirements but the most common is polyurethane foam. This is an open cell foam and must be protected from soaking up water by a covering of plastic coated nylon. Closed cell foams would be waterproof in themselves but they have one common disadvantage. When they have been compressed for any length of time, they collapse and do not spring back. These foam materials may be built right into the sleeping bag, or they may be used as a separate pad. If the padding is going into the bag itself, a long staple wool or Dacron II batt is a good material to use because it has a softer feel and stuffs in a stuff sack better.

The most insulation and comfort for the least amount of bulk and weight is supplied by a 36″ x 20″ pad of 1½″ polyurethane foam. This is sufficient to reach from hips to shoulders. By making a pillow of your clothing inside the sleeper stuff sack and putting your feet up on an empty pack you will have enough insulation even for winter use. Since polyurethane is an open cell foam it will act like a sponge in the presence of moisture so it must be protected by a waterproof covering. To make such a foam pad back packable, it is carried in the same stuff sack as the sleeping bag. This may sound impossible, but if the sack is about 10″ in diameter, and the rolled up pad is placed in first and allowed to expand to the outside, the sleeping bag can be stuffed down inside the pad, compressing it against the stuff sack until you have one compact bundle containing more sleeping comfort in less space than any other combination.

The question of thickness in a sleeping bag depends upon the temperature at which it is to be used and upon the kind of sleep wanted. Strange as it may seem, experiments have shown that it is possible to get a good night's rest even though sleep itself comes only fitfully. If a bag is generally warm but one or two pressure points get cold enough to cause wakefulness, merely turning over and starting again can provide a night's rest that is satisfactory from a recuperative standpoint. Of course, the more the cold spots are reduced the longer the uninterrupted slumber. For a full night's comfortable sleep a much heavier sleeping bag is needed than for a night of recuperative rest. This problem is important only at winter temperatures or at very high altitude.

According to A. C. Burton's *Man in a Cold Environment*, a sleeping man requires approximately the thickness of insulation shown in the following table for a good night's sleep at various temperatures. This thickness is measured from the skin to the outer surface of the bag, including the air trapped between the various layers of clothing, which can account for up to 1″ of the thickness required, if the clothing is dry.

40°	1½″ of insulation
20°	2″ of insulation
0°	2½″ of insulation
−20°	3″ of insulation
−40°	3½″ of insulation

We have discussed the insulating materials in theory. When they are actually incorporated into a sleeping bag there are many factors that detract from their theoretical performance furnishing a certain thickness of dead air space. The heavier and stiffer the shell fabric, for instance, the more insulating material will be needed to push the fabric out to the desired thickness. Thus, the lightest fabrics consistent with durability should be used, particularly for the top of the bag.

There are two types of sleeping bag construction, "space filler" and "differential cut," and the choice between them depends mostly on your sleeping habits. A rectangular sleeping bag or two singles that zip together to make a double, give lots of room and freedom, but are really inefficient. These should be of space filler construction; that is, everything should be designed to help fill up the inside of the bag so the sleeper won't have a lot of circulating air to warm. These bags are cut as a flat quilt and wrapped around to form a bag. Their outside is stretched tight and the inside hangs in loose, space filling folds.

However, if an elbow or knee, or buttocks is pressed against the bag from inside there is nothing to prevent compression of the down against the outer layer, forming a cold spot. In a close fitting mummy bag this becomes more important, so the differential cut is used. That means the inner and outer layers are cut as cylinders of different diameters. When properly made the outer layer remains loose and insulating even when the inner layer is stretched tight by a knee, etc. See Figs. 3 and 4, Plate VI, p. 77. The amount of differential between outer and inner is shown in the following table.

Table of Differential Cuts—in Inches

If bag thickness is	½	1	1½	2	2½	3
cut the outer circumference this much larger than the inner	3⅛	6¼	9¾	12½	15½	19

An efficient bag should be made to the dimensions of the person or persons using it. These dimensions will differ considerably even though two people may be the same size, because they may have different sleeping habits. The person using the bag should determine his space requirements —is he a thrasher or a quiet sleeper, does he need knee or shoulder space or will he be comfortable in a tighter form fitting bag? This is the *space* that should be measured when the size of the bag is being determined. A piece of string should be passed around the body lengthwise, going the maximum distance around the feet. The string should then be pulled as loose as desired for the *inside* fabric of the bag. This will give the total length which must be designed into the *inside* layer of the bag. The same technique is used to get the proper circumference around the shoulders and hips.

Another problem in making a low temperature sleeping bag is quilting, or forming compartments to contain the down. Obviously stitching the outer and inner layers of fabric together not only puts holes in the fabric through which warm air can pass, but reduces the thickness to almost nothing, thus eliminating the insulation at the stitching.

In making a bag using Dacron batts it is difficult to avoid the stitch-through construction. However, since Dacron is more suitable for summer bags at medium temperatures anyway, a sandwich of Dacron batting between two layers of nylon works out very well. A differential cut allowing for about 1″ thickness should be used for a 2-pound batt. If a slightly warmer Dacron bag is desired, stitching through all layers can be avoided by making two separately quilted layers, one a sandwich of the outer layer of fabric and a layer of cheesecloth and another sandwich of the inner layer of fabric and a layer of cheesecloth. The quilting stitching on the inner layer should be offset from that of the outer. To prevent too much interaction or rubbing between the layers a couple of gussets can be sewn into adjacent seams when quilting and eventually sewn together before completion of the bag. (See Fig. 5, Plate VI, p. 77.) In lengthwise quilting the differential is accommodated by spacing the quilting lines farther apart on the outer fabric than on the inner.

It is generally a good idea to use down for bags other than summer weight as sufficient thickness of Dacron adds quite a lot of weight and bulk. The two advantages of Dacron are low cost and more retention of its insulating thickness when wet.

Down, or down and feathers, are handled quite differently from Dacron or other batting. The tubes or compartments are formed first and then the insulation is carefully measured out and blown or placed by hand in each compartment. Here again the problem is to maintain the desired thickness of insulation. The efficiency of down as insulation is largely wasted if the stitched through construction is used, as discussed above. There isn't even the thickness of the compressed batt at the stitching, as with Dacron, only the two layers of light fabric are left at the seams. Even worse, the down tends to be held away from these seams for an inch or so on each side.

There are two common methods of avoiding this undesirable stitched-through construction. One is cutting strips of fabric as wide as the bag is to be thick, plus allowing for seams on each edge. These strips or gussets are then sewn one edge to the outer fabric and one edge to the inner fabric forming box tubes to hold the down. The second method is the use of a third layer of fabric, or diaphragm, which can be nylon netting or some such light material. The use of nylon netting will eliminate the disappointment of having the inside of the bag come apart long before the rest of the bag is worn out. Nettings are good too because the down tends to get stuck in them and this retards shifting. This third layer of fabric is sewn alternately to first the inner then the outer layer of fabric forming triangular sectioned, overlapping tubes. One advantage of this method of diaphragm construction using overlapping tubes is that the natural tendency of the down to pull away from all such partitions, a fact which is actually visible in a gusseted bag, is offset by the fact that the thin spot on one tube is under the thickest part of another. (See Fig. 6, Plate VI, p. 77.)

If for some reason, lengthwise tubes must be used in a sleeping bag, the gusseted construction should be used because the diaphragm construction does not allow the differential cut to shift to a pushed out spot when needed. Where possible, tubes running around the bag should be used and here the more efficient diaphragm construction may be used.

To accommodate the differential cut in tubes running around the bag the diaphragm must be cut the length of the *outer* fabric of the bag and gathered as it is sewn to the inner fabric so it comes out even with the smaller circumference of the *inner* fabric. It is a good idea to key mark center and quarters of the three layers to make sure the gathering is evenly spaced around the bag.

The desired thickness of the bag is governed more by the spacing of the diaphragm or gusset seams (width of tube) than anything else. These tables are the result of extensive research on experimental compartments filled with the least practical amount of down.

The Resulting Thickness Using Minimum
Amounts of Down, for 2 Constructions
Compiled by GERRY

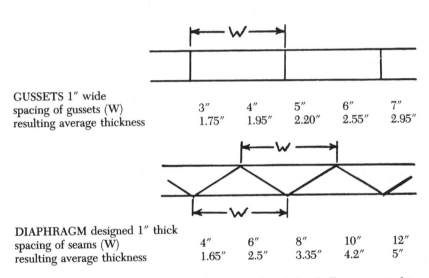

GUSSETS 1″ wide					
spacing of gussets (W)	3″	4″	5″	6″	7″
resulting average thickness	1.75″	1.95″	2.20″	2.55″	2.95″

DIAPHRAGM designed 1″ thick					
spacing of seams (W)	4″	6″	8″	10″	12″
resulting average thickness	1.65″	2.5″	3.35″	4.2″	5″

Once the thickness of the bag is determined and the shell constructed to these dimensions, consideration must be given to the amount of down required to fill the compartments to this thickness. A good grade of goose down will fill about 500 cubic inches per ounce. However, this is a theoretical minimum and is practical only in very small compartments. In larger compartments or long tubes, such a small amount of down will shift and leave cold spots. A practical minimum amount of down would be just enough so the down won't settle when the compartments are lightly shaken in a vertical position. However, this means you must actively redistribute and fluff the down each time you use the bag, such as a bird preens its down in cold weather. To put enough down in a bag so you won't have to bother with distribution, try the pat test. Put enough down in each compartment so that when you pat it with your hand, you completely compress one spot and when your hand is removed, the spot quickly regains its thickness. Do not put in more than this, as you are just adding weight and expense, not warmth. Overstuffing a bag with down adds nothing but more weight and bulk. It is the thickness that counts.

The bottom of a bag should never be overstuffed with down. Down will take three times the weight of foam or other suitable material to make the bottom of the sleeping bag warm. This is due to the compressibility of the down. It will not support the body's weight and thin cold spots will result.

The amount of padding used in the bottom of a sleeping bag is limited by the desired size—usually small—of the rolled bag. The padding used for support is of course non-compressible and too much will make a bulky bag. As much as is compatible with the rolled size of the bag should be used. Any extra amount under shoulders, hips, and feet will be an advantage for comfort and insulation.

In making a bag with a padded bottom it is convenient to encase the entire bottom in a coated waterproof fabric. A single coated fabric (one side only coated) should be used with the fabric side out (next to the sleeper) and the coated side in (next to the insulation). The entire bottom of the sleeping bag, inner and outer layers, should be encased with coated fabric. This keeps both body moisture, one pint per night, and outside moisture from entering the insulation of the padded bottom. It is even possible to avoid stitching through the outer layer of the bottom by using a layer of nylon netting inside to form compartments for the padding. (See Fig. 7, Plate VI, p. 77.) An air escape hole must be put in the inner fabric or it will be impossible to roll the bag up due to the trapped air in the mattress. If a vapor barrier mattress such as this is used, the top two-thirds of the bag must be of permeable fabric.

An excellent and versatile combination is an all down filled sleeping bag of light weight, which is good by itself in summer, and a nylon cover shell incorporating insulating mattress pads for winter use. The head can be a compartment to hold extra clothes to form a pillow. Below the pads, pants or other heavy clothing can be used inside the cover shell to extend the insulation. If the shell has a coated fabric bottom it makes a dry safe place to keep clothes during the night without actually taking them into the sleeping bag. (See Fig. 8, Plate VI, p. 77.) This combination can be used with a down jacket and waist length down bag for sleeping at temperatures down to at least zero.

The trickiest part of making a down filled item is the handling of the down.

DOWN BLOWING

In filling a sleeping bag or down filled garment, the first consideration is to divide the down between the various tubes or compartments by

WEIGHT. As little as 1 ounce will fill 500 cubic inches and yet 6 ounces can be easily compressed into the same space, so obviously it is practically impossible to guess at equal amounts of down by volume or feel. Scales accurate to $\frac{1}{4}$ ounce are desirable. If the tubes are uniform as to cross section the down can be apportioned according to length only. If they are not uniform some rule of thumb adjustments are necessary. To be safe you can hold back a small bit of down for adjustment in case some of the tubes come out short. The scales should be fitted with a 1 cubic foot open box of heavy paper and the weight of the box subtracted at each weighing. The proper amount is the minimum quantity which will not settle down when the tubes are held vertically and shaken.

The down can be put in the weighing box by handfuls, grabbing each handful in the down, compressing it, and tucking in all the loose pieces before transferring it to the scales. If the movements are slow the mess stays localized. A vacuum cleaner can be used to pick the down out of the weighing box and blow it into the tubes. The tube must be well secured around the exhaust of the vacuum before turning it on. As tubes are filled, roll the ends shut and pin. The down can also be placed by hand, using the same method as used for weighing. In fact it is easier and safer to do small compartments by hand.

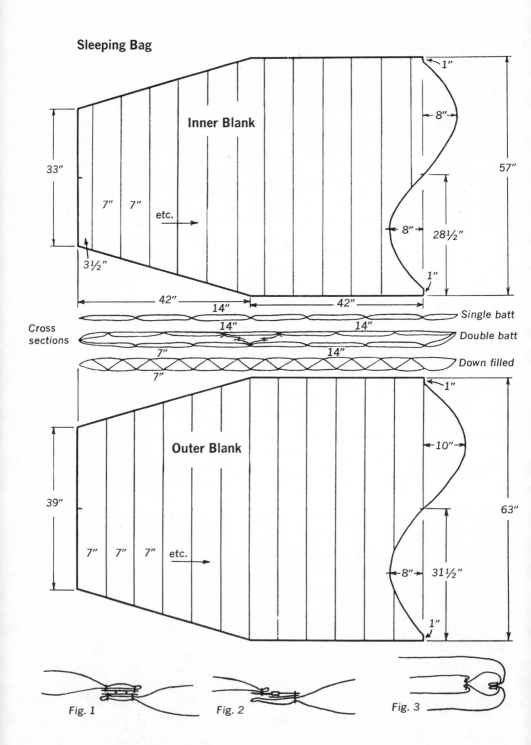

Sleeping Bag

Inner Blank

33"

7" 7" etc.

3½"

1"

8"

8"

28½"

57"

1"

42"

14"

42"

14"

14"

Cross sections

Single batt

Double batt

Down filled

7"

14"

7"

Outer Blank

39"

7" 7" 7" etc.

1"

10"

8"

31½"

63"

1"

Fig. 1

Fig. 2

Fig. 3

SLEEPING BAG

LIST OF MATERIALS

Single Dacron Batt
Fabric—6½ yards 39" or 6 yards 42"
Dacron—one 1 pound batt
Nylon lace—4 yards
Leather grommet—1
Velcro tape—42" and 8 Dot Snappers; or one 42" zipper

Double Dacron Batt
Fabric—6½ yards 39" or 6 yards 42"
Cheesecloth—6 yards 36"
Dacron—two 1 pound batts
Nylon lace—4 yards
Leather grommet—1
Velcro tape—42" and 8 Dot Snappers; or one 42" zipper

Down Filled
Fabric—6½ yards 39" or 6 yards 42"
Nylon mosquito netting—4 yards 44"
Down—1 pound
Nylon lace—4 yards
Leather grommet—1
Velcro tape—42" and 8 Dot Snappers; or one 42" zipper

INSTRUCTIONS

I. Read "Patterns and Sewing" to familiarize yourself with the terms and operations used.

II. Lay out pieces

(a) Alterations: this bag will fit seventy-five per cent of the male population but it is best to check the size before starting to cut. Pin a sheet to the inner bag size and crawl in. To make the circumference larger simply add the required inches to both inner and outer diagrams. For the curve of the hood add ¼ of the increase to each station. To change the length either longer or shorter, leave the tube spacing the same and cut off or lengthen the foot end. However, keep the width of the foot as indicated. If this makes the taper appear too abrupt or too long, move up the point of taper half as much as the length was changed. If the bag is lengthened more than 3", add another tube. If a tapered foot is not wanted, the foot end can be made rectangular without difficulty. The opening is made at the side so it can be left open for ventilation while the bag still covers the occupant. If zip-together, matching bags are desired they must be mirror images of one another. To make the easiest bag possible, the single batt bag may be cut the same width outside as inside. This saves a good deal of trouble in sewing the quilting.

(b) Cut fabric as long as the bag is wide and piece to length crosswise of the bag, starting at the foot end. Usually only 2 full widths of fabric are needed to make the length, and the hood flap can be pieced on from scraps. The inner and outer tapered pieces may be cut next to each other to prevent waste. Use a hem seam to join the pieces. Make one outer blank and one inner blank, being sure that when they are placed together the rough sides of the piecing seams lie between the two blanks.

(c) In marking out the curves make them as smooth as possible but they are not critical as long as the beginning and ending points indicated are accurate.

(d) Mark the quilting or tube lines. For a down filled bag mark on the "between" sides of the inner and outer blanks. The lines are 7" apart. For a 2 batt Dacron bag, mark on the outsides of the inner and outer blanks, using every other line from the outer diagram or just twice the spacing as for a down bag. For a single batt Dacron bag, use the same spacing as indicated for the Dacron outer blank of the double bag. Use chalk to mark outside of bag so it will brush off. For all types of bag, mark a center line where it crosses each tube mark and the head of foot edges.

(e) Cut the blanks to size and shape allowing about ½" for seams.

III. Install insulation

(a) Single Dacron Batt

1. Spread out the outer blank on a clean bare floor (not a rug) or table, marked side down. Unfold a 2-pound Dacron batt on top of this and pull out till it covers all of the blank. Trim edges of the batt until it matches the blank. Use the scraps to pad out the hip, shoulder, and foot areas (in that order of importance).

2. Place the inner blank on top of this sandwich, centered sidewise between the edges of the wider outer blank. Pin through all three layers at the center marks of each tube line. Ease half the surplus of the outer blank and the batting toward the center pins and pin again at the quarters of each tube line. Then pin the ends of each tube line so inner and outer and batt all come out even.

3. Sew along the tube lines with the longest possible stitch and loosest

possible tensions. Ease the surplus outer blank and the batting into the seam so it is all gone by the time each pin is reached. Remove pins as they are reached. The technique for getting all layers through the machine is to smooth the layers and pull firmly with one hand as the bag goes through the machine.

(b) Double Dacron Batts

1. Proceed as for step no. 1 under Single Dacron Batt, using one of the batts. However, two batts are quite bulky so go easy on the padding with scraps.
2. Proceed as for step no. 1 but using the inner blank and the other batt. Don't do any padding. In fact, to reduce bulk this batt can be stopped at the bottom of the S curve of the top edge.
3. Cover each blank and batt combination with a layer of cheesecloth. Trim cloth to shape and if it doesn't reach full width, don't worry. Pin along the tube marks, using safety pins. If it can be managed, stitch along the tube lines with the fabric side up and the cheesecloth down. Otherwise just sew on top of the cheesecloth being very careful that the presser foot doesn't get caught in the cheesecloth and batting. Use the longest stitch possible and loosest tensions.
4. To prevent too much interaction between the inner and outer quilt, sew a couple of anchor strips in the center tube seams. Strips of any light fabric 2″ wide will do. Sew 2 by their centers in one seam of the outer quilt and sew 4 by their ends in the adjacent seams of the inner quilt spaced to match. These will be joined later. See cross section of the Double Dacron Batt bag.

(c) Down Filled

1. Piece together and cut a blank of nylon mosquito netting the same shape as the outer blank and mark both outer and inner tube lines on it, including center marks.
2. Sew this netting diaphragm alternately to the lines on the inner and outer blanks. In sewing it to the inner blank, the netting must be tucked at frequent intervals so the center marks, and eventually the ends of both pieces come out even.
3. Starting on the edge of the bag, 4″ short of the last tube seam, sew across the top edge with a single stitch about ¼″ in, tucking the outer, so center and end marks come out even with the inner. Continue sewing down the pointed side and across the foot but using a finished hem seam. The outer must be tucked across the foot to come out even.
4. Fill the tubes with down. Place one fistful way down in each tube,

withdrawing the hand slowly. Repeat with a second and third handful, until all tubes have the same number of handfuls in proportion to their length. For example, 6 each in the longest, tapering to 3 in the shortest. Clothespins to close each tube as the down is inserted will help keep the mess under control. When almost all the down is used up, pin each tube closed and fluff up the bag to distribute the down. Hold the bag up so the tubes are vertical with a very strong light behind it. Shake until it can be seen that the down has settled in some of the tubes. Place additional down in these tubes, fluff up, and shake again. Repeat this until all tubes are filled the same, and the down is all used up. Be sure to fluff up each time. The tubes up in the hood may be half filled to save down. By weight, the down figures about $^{11}/_{16}$ ounce in the longest tubes to $^3/_8$ ounce at the foot, and about $^1/_4$ ounce in the hood flap tubes.

5. Now close this side of the bag with a finished hem seam.

IV. Finish details

(a) To finish the single batt Dacron bag, sew across the head with a single stitched plain seam, tucking the outer blank to come out even. Sew down one side, across the foot, tucking the outer fabric, and up the other side with a finished hem seam. For the double batt bag, place both quilts together, cheesecloth to cheesecloth and sew the anchor strips together so the quilts are held in position. Now sew around the edges just as in the single batt bag. The down bag is already finished to this point.

(b) Cut and piece a facing type of drawhem for the top edge of the bag and in its center sew a leather grommet where the drawstrings can come out. Install across the top of the bag with the drawstrings securely anchored at the ends.

(c) The bag may be closed with either a zipper or Velcro tape. In either case, an overlap is used and this is carried down to the foot of the bag with a double row of stitching below the Velcro or zipper.

Velcro tape—Set matching snaps about 6" apart in the 2 lengths of tape and then sew the tapes to the facing surfaces of the bag. Sew the hook tape to the outside of the edge of the bag bottom and sew the loop tape to the inside edge of the bag top. Be sure the snaps all match up perfectly. Sew both edges of the tape. To close, simply snap the snaps and the tape will stick together by itself. See Fig. 1, p. 86.

Zippers—Sew one half to the inside of the top so the teeth extend past the bag fabric. Sew the other side to the outside of the bottom about 1½" in so a flap will extend over the zipper teeth on the inside. It is a good idea to include a tape between the zipper and the bag to help avoid snagging.

In both cases continue the overlap of the bag down past the closure to the foot and stitch twice about $\frac{1}{2}''$ apart.

(d) To close the foot, turn the bag inside out. Fold end closed vertically and stitch just inside the edge. About 2" from each end include the center of a couple of tie tapes 36" long so their ends will be outside the bag when it is right side out and so that two little loops will be inside the bag. These are handy to tie down a liner sheet if one is used. To stitch out this cold seam across the foot of the bag, pinch up the fabric about 1" back from the first row of stitching and pull out together. Barely catch these folds in another row of stitching as shown in Fig. 3, p. 86. This row of stitching can also be carried up the side to meet the closure but will use up 2" of the inside circumference.

CHAPTER VI TENTS

Leaving out the circus and carnival variety, on the subject of tents there are almost as many opinions as there are tents. Tents range in size from the size of a summer cottage to a little tent which is scarcely more than a sleeping bag cover. We assume here that the tent is for backpacking which automatically eliminates about ninety-eight per cent of all tents. This does not mean that it need be a tiny flimsy affair, however. Careful choice of materials can provide a tent with a surprising amount of space.

The tents described will be of two main types. The first will be the tent used primarily for shelter from rain and insects in the forest, or at least under moderate temperature conditions. The second type is the tent to be used primarily above timberline, often on snow, winter or summer, under severe climatic conditions. Naturally, each tent can invade the other's domain—will in fact often be required to do so. However, in choosing the design for a tent its main use must be determined and a design chosen which best fulfills this purpose. Using it under other conditions will necessitate compromises.

FOREST TENTS

The forest tent can be the lightest possible because it can be made without a floor, it need not close up completely and a single layer of fabric will usually suffice. Some campers even prefer a light tarp to a tent due to the many ways in which a tarp can be pitched to suit conditions. The tarp, however, generally requires more fabric per square foot of coverage than a tent cut specifically for one of these shapes.

The weight of a tent will depend almost entirely on the yardage of fabric it requires. The greatest amount of volume enclosed by the least surface area is accomplished by a sphere, but although there have been several attempts to make hemispherical tents, the weight of the accouterments necessary to hold this shape has been excessive in small structures. The same is true in semicylindrical shapes such as a quonset hut, but one or two practical solutions have been used with high altitude tents and will be mentioned later.

Next to the semicylindrical shape in volume enclosed per square yard of fabric is the conical shape. This at once brings to mind the tepee of the Indians. In fact there is no tent which will put so much area under cover with so little fabric as a tepee. However, in most areas, it is no longer possible to cut the poles it requires.

Next to the tepee in space enclosed is the square pyramidal tent variously known as the "Miner's Tent," "Herder Tent," etc. (See Fig. 1, Plate VII, p. 94.) This usually requires only a single center pole and can be made any size from 7' x 7' to 14' x 14'. Of the usual backpacking tents this design puts the greatest area under cover for the least amount of fabric. It is also a very stable design in high wind due to the fact that all the walls slope and spill the wind. The steep pitch of the walls means that it will also shed rain efficiently. Interior space can also be enlarged if a pull-out is attached a little way up each center seam. These should not be pulled out too tight, just enough to pull out the natural sag. Side walls and other variations can be applied to the basic design.

The Hill and Dale Tent is a variation of the square pyramidal tent, though at first sight it might not appear so. It is approximately one half of the pyramid with a little bit of the other half forming a weather hood over the open side. This makes a lean-to tent with one full side open to the fire but it uses less fabric than a conventional lean-to and is simpler to pitch, requiring only a single pole. The hood gives considerable weather protection and a floor can be sewn in that will also zip partway up the front opening to close it off even further, making it completely weather tight and still allowing plenty of ventilation. This design makes one of the roomiest and lightest tents possible. (See Fig. 2, Plate VII, p. 94.)

The number of tent designs is legion, therefore we will confine ourselves here to describing those that we feel are best for a particular situation and with which we have had the most experience. The omission of a design does not mean it is no good, and there will be enough information included in the construction details so that a tent of any design can be constructed.

Sometimes a tent must be versatile because of changing weather conditions and variation in number of people it must accommodate. One of the most flexible designs and one of the easiest to make is the Combination Lean-to Tent. Pitched as a lean-to it will accommodate four people and present an open front to the fire with well enclosed ends. With the fly closed down it will hold two and is completely weatherproof. Between these two extremes there is the vestibule arrangement with one end closed down and the other open, which could sleep three, and the common "pup tent" arrangement which is also wide enough for three. (See Fig. 3, Plate VII, p. 94.)

The lightest possible tent is one which is cut to fit the occupants.

PLATE VII

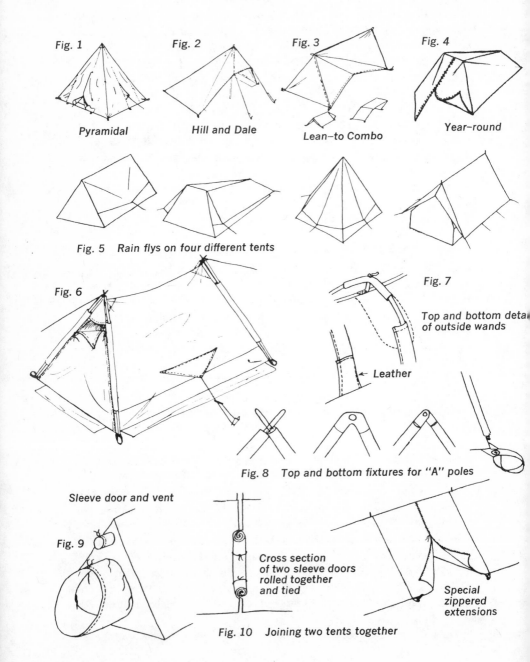

Fig. 1   Pyramidal

Fig. 2   Hill and Dale

Fig. 3   Lean–to Combo

Fig. 4   Year–round

Fig. 5   Rain flys on four different tents

Fig. 6

Fig. 7   Top and bottom detail of outside wands

Leather

Fig. 8   Top and bottom fixtures for "A" poles

Sleeve door and vent

Fig. 9

Cross section of two sleeve doors rolled together and tied

Special zippered extensions

Fig. 10   Joining two tents together

Primarily this means tapering one end to take the feet. The end can thus be only about 18″ high, and if mummy shape sleeping bags are used it can also be only 2 to 2½ feet wide. The head end should be ample for two shoulders in width and high enough to sit up comfortably. Some additional room is usually required to keep the packs and gear under cover during inclement weather. A one-man tent can be a little narrower but not too much weight can be saved here.

The Year-round Tent is of this tapered design and has proven to be the most popular two-man tent since the Army Pup Tent. One improvement it has over the usual tent is an extra, zippered hood, entirely outside the floored area and separated from it by a sill. The zipper runs up the ridge so that one half can be left staked out for wind protection and the other used as the door. At night there is room for all your gear under cover. The second improvement over the usual design is the cross ridge at the top which gives more head room than the usual small tent with side walls coming together in a point at the top. With a sewn-in floor this tent can be closed up tight enough for occasional use on snow or above timberline. (See Fig. 4, Plate VII, p. 94.)

Any of the above described tents can be fitted easily with mosquito netting for keeping out insects. Nylon netting cut to fit over the open door is slit up the center and a size 3 zipper installed. When sewing the edges around the door, include a couple of 18″ lengths of lace along the sides to tie the netting back out of the way when it's not needed. To get a mosquito-proof seal across the floor, cut the netting 6″ to 10″ too long. This is lighter and more convenient in small tents than two more zippers. This flap provides plenty of overlap to keep the mosquitoes out. If the bugs are the really eager kind, gaining entrance through the ground, or if the ground is damp, a floor can be sewn or snapped into any of these tents. A tent with a floor is easier to pitch since the exact shape for staking out is determined by the floor. Tents without floors or with snap-in floors should have a 6″ to 10″ wide flap inside all around the bottom edges with sewn mitered corners to prevent gaps and drafts along the ground.

WATER REPELLENCY

The problem of water repellency in a tent deserves special consideration along with problems of condensation—a problem of great importance in any fully enclosed tent. In using a tarp as a tent a plastic or neoprene coated fabric can be used since there will be enough ventilation. Coated fabrics have the disadvantage of wearing and cracking. When the coating is worn off there is nothing but a flimsy nylon fabric left. If the worn spot isn't large it can be repaired by recoating with a vinyl base cement or lacquer which is available in most plastics shops.

One way to beat the water repellency problem in small tents is to use a rain fly. This fly is pitched over the tent proper, giving protection to the tent from the direct force of the rain. The fly can be of the lightest plastic coated nylon material.

The fly can be entirely separate from the tent or it can be an integral part of it, utilizing the same poles and stakes to pitch it, though separate stakes give more clearance. The fly need not cover every square foot of the tent. If the eaves are out far enough so the run off doesn't pour onto the tent they can be quite a bit shorter in length than the sides of the tent.

If there is danger of splashing or if the tent is very small so that sleeping bags are bound to rub the insides of the fabric, the lower walls can be faced inside with a light weight single coated fabric. This makes a completely waterproof lower portion while still leaving it free to breathe, thus reducing condensation. (See Fig. 5, Plate VII, p. 94.) If the tent has a vestibule or porch fly of some sort, there is little need to design the rain fly to cover any but that portion of the tent occupied by the sleeping gear. Generally speaking the rain fly is the best way to get a really waterproof tent and reduce condensation. Both tent and fly should be of light weight nylon (the fly coated and the tent breathable) with a saving in weight and increase in strength over a single layer of cotton.

Another way to be sure of good wet weather protection is to use a 5 ounce tightly woven cotton fabric. This will take and retain almost any kind of water repellent treatment and hold it for an entire season. Protection from rain, however, is only one of the three protections you want from a tent. The others are wind protection, which means capability of complete closure, and protection from insects, which means all openings for ventilation covered by nylon mosquito netting and sewn in floor.

HIGH ALTITUDE TENTS

The second type of tent to be discussed is the high altitude tent, or those tents which are used on snow and in severe weather. They differ from forest tents in that they must close absolutely tight so wind blown snow will not sift in and so that heat can be conserved. Consideration must be given to this all important conservation of heat. Important details such as arrangements for getting in and out of the tent with bulky clothing, cooking with a gasoline stove inside the tent, drying and storing wet gear and clothing apart from the sleeping equipment, must all receive attention. In some cases stability in a high wind is of special importance since flapping tent walls can make it impossible to cook and sleep for days at a time. Visibility of the tent from a distance can be extremely important. Needless to say, no compromise with the very finest materials and construction features should be made in tents for use under extreme conditions.

The simplest high altitude tent design is an "A" shape with sewn in floor, ends closed with sleeve doors, and poles along the sides of the "A" at each end. If the ends are slanted in toward one another at the top they not only spill the wind better but also allow a longer floor with a shorter ridge that is less likely to sag. Pull out flaps on the sides will give a lot more room in the tent by eliminating sag and they will also increase the stability in a wind. (See Fig. 6, Plate VII, p. 94.)

Flexible wands, one or two, in the center of the tent may be used to eliminate sag and decrease the flapping of tent sides. The wands are almost like another "A" pole as used at each end except that they are spread at a much wider angle than the tent itself at the top and are pulled in at the bottom to conform to the width of the tent floor, thus forming a gothic arch shape with lots of interior room and a good deal less flapping in the wind. The wands can be used either inside the tent, held in position by a loop in the ridge and one near the floor on each side with suitable reinforcing to prevent the lower ends from wearing through the walls, or they can be inserted in a special sleeve sewn to the outside of the tent. (See Fig. 7, Plate VII, p. 94.)

The "A" poles at either end should have their tops joined securely together forming the most rigid bracing possible, a triangle. Several methods of joining the tops of the poles are illustrated. The poles themselves are attached to the tent by passing them through sleeves sewn into the end seams. This eliminates any sagging of the tent between the top and bottom of the poles.

Anything exerting a steady pressure on snow will tend to sink down through it. For this reason the bottoms of tent poles should be fastened to the corners of the tent. This makes the entire tent an integral unit and although the whole tent will sink eventually the poles will not disappear the first night out. One of the simplest ways of anchoring the bottoms of the poles to the tent is to combine a grommet with the peg loop to accept a short prong in the bottom of the pole. (See Fig. 8, Plate VII, p. 94.)

Many times a high altitude tent must be pitched on rocky ground where it is impossible to drive stakes, or in such soft snow that even broad snow stakes won't take hold. In this situation it is handy to have a flap about 9″ wide running around the entire tent. Rocks or snow can be piled on the flap to hold the tent in position. If wind is allowed to get under the floor of the tent the whole thing, occupants and all, is apt to go blowing across the ground or down the gulch. Even when stakes are well driven it is a good idea to weight this flap to keep the wind from under the floor. When the tent is dug into the snow, however, these flaps should be tucked under the tent if they are not needed since melt water will run down and freeze them in solidly if they are left out. Since this sometimes happens in spite of preventive measures the flap should be made of a plastic coated nylon so it doesn't absorb water before freezing in. If they have to be cut off to free the tent, they can be replaced easily. All peg loops should be on top of the snow flaps in order to allow the flaps to be tucked under the tent.

Snow melt water can be a problem with a tent set up on snow for any length of time. To help alleviate the inconvenience of moisture coming through where sleeping bags touch the walls the lower 8″ or 9″ of the tent wall can be protected by a strip of coated fabric. The lightest single coat will do if the coating is sandwiched between its own base fabric and the tent wall. The coated fabric should be sewn to the inside of the tent so there won't be any seam on the outside to catch run off water and shunt it into the tent. It should not be used in place of the tent fabric.

If it is likely that the occupants of a tent are to be shut up for several days of stormy weather adequate means of ventilation must be provided. A means of opening both ends of the tent can be provided, and at least one of these openings should be in the peak to provide ventilation for the cooking done directly under it. If the cooking is done in front of the door it is convenient to have another door at the opposite end so the cook won't be trampled by his companions going in and out. It's nice to be able to cook directly on the ground or snow rather than the tent floor since stew and sleeping bags make a gooey mixture. A zippered hole in the floor (two 18-inch zippers meeting at the top of a triangle will usually be sufficient) provides a spot for the stove and kettle to sit. This hole also prevents any spilled fuel from becoming a fire hazard except locally on the bare ground.

An added advantage to having a tent with two doors is that two tents can frequently be set up joined together by one set of doors making living much more agreeable for their joint occupants. If the storm sleeve type of door is used these can be joined successfully if the tie tapes used to tie them open are at least six in number and are in the same position on each tent. The outside tapes of each tent are tied together closely, then the two sleeves are rolled up together in one roll making a weatherproof joint. The inside tapes are then tied together to hold the rolled sleeves. If it is known that tents are usually going to be used together it may be worthwhile to sew an extension 1½ to 2 feet long to the ends of the tents with 2 halves of a separating zipper sewn along the edge of each extension. The flaps are zipped together to form an entrance vestibule or cooking room between the two tents. (See Fig. 10, Plate VII, p. 94.)

Ingenious use of a two-way zipper with several sliders can be made to meet various situations. If the tent is to be used occasionally below timberline where a wood fire can be enjoyed it is a great comfort to have the door in one end consist of a couple of zippers down each side, so that the end opens up completely. This arrangement can be used at high altitudes where condensation is a problem, but many climbers consider the possible failure of a zipper too much of a chance to take. When the zipper is used with a vestibule (discussed below), zipper failure is not so critical. If the simple zipper door is used in one end, this is also a means of joining two tents together if separating zippers are used. This type of door provides easy ventilation from the peak of the tent when a small hood is sewn over the outside to keep out the snow and rain.

VESTIBULES

A vestibule, or separate entry, which gives a space entirely separate from the main sleeping area for storing wet and snowy gear and for cooking, is a feature well worth considering. If the size of the tent already includes the extra area, the added weight consists only of an inner curtain, zipper, and sill which divide the vestibule from the rest of the tent. Sometimes the vestibule is added on outside the regular end of the tent and can be rolled back and tied up when not in use. When this arrangement is used there are large overlapping flaps instead of a floor at the bottom edges of the vestibule sections. It will probably have two halves joined by a zipper down the ridge between them. One half is staked out permanently, the other half will be used as the door. In other cases the vestibule is the real end of the tent and a light inner curtain is used to separate it from the rest of the tent. This is true if the double walled tent is used. (See Fig. 1, Plate VIII, p. 100.)

DOUBLE WALLS

A double walled tent is actually a tent within a tent. Its purpose is the conservation of heat. It does this by using the outer tent fabric to break the force of the wind, with a lighter inner liner keeping the occupants out of contact with the cold outer walls. In order for the two walls to do this efficiently there must be a clear passage for the air between the two walls from the windward to the leeward side of the tent. This air between the walls is not insulation in the usual sense since it is by no means dead air. Rather, the space is used to cut down the forced air penetration present with any porous fabric when there is wind pressure on one side and not on the other. Normally in a single wall tent the cold wind filters in the windward side and a like amount of warm air filters out the leeward side. In a proper double walled tent the cold air comes in the windward side

PLATE VIII

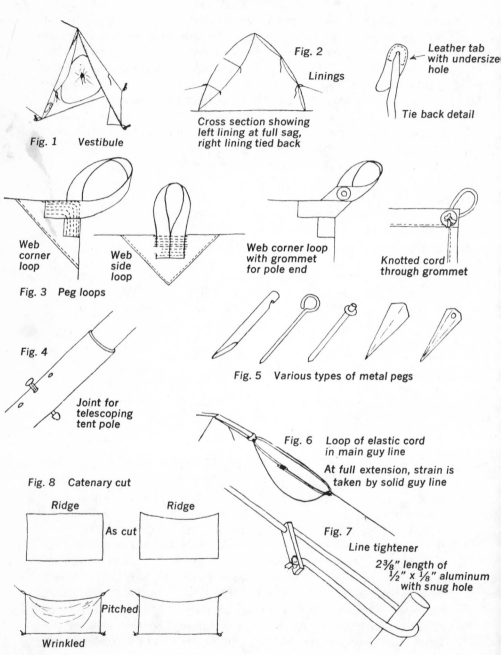

Fig. 1   Vestibule

Fig. 2   Linings

Cross section showing
left lining at full sag,
right lining tied back

Leather tab
with undersize
hole

Tie back detail

Fig. 3   Peg loops

Web
corner
loop

Web
side
loop

Web corner loop
with grommet
for pole end

Knotted cord
through grommet

Fig. 4

Joint for
telescoping
tent pole

Fig. 5   Various types of metal pegs

Fig. 6   Loop of elastic cord
in main guy line

At full extension, strain is
taken by solid guy line

Fig. 8   Catenary cut

Ridge

Ridge

As cut

Pitched

Wrinkled

Fig. 7

Line tightener

2⅜" length of
½" x ⅛" aluminum
with snug hole

and passes around the inner tent, exerting very little pressure on it, and then passes out through the leeward side. The warm air remains undisturbed inside the inner tent.

If the tent is made double walled in panels, with no escape for the incoming cold air, the cold air will be forced to pass through the inner layer into the warm interior. Double layers would increase the resistance to air passage but would not be as efficient as the use of the tent within a tent allowing air to pass through between the layers.

Since the inner layer of a double tent is subject to much less wind pressure than the outer wall, it can be made of the very lightest material.

The suspension of the inner tent inside the outer can be a source of much confusion and should be kept as simple as possible. Sewing or snapping the two walls together around the floor helps to make a simple unit of the two tents. If the tent is of the ordinary "A" shape, the ridge of the inner tent can be stretched and held by two straps and buckles, or tie cords, from the peaks of the outer tent. The outer tent is generally the one pitched, with the liner suspended inside from it. If wands are used they will tend to give plenty of space between inner and outer tents because the sag of the outer wall will be pulled out and the inner will sag in slightly. This is fine for sleeping and keeping warm because it reduces the amount of area inside the tent to be heated. However, for other operations it cramps the space and it is a good idea to use a couple of tie-backs along each spreader wand to pull the sag of the liner up to meet the outer wall. These tie-backs can be pieces of cotton lace sewn to the outer fabric at the same time the outside sleeves for the wands are sewn on so that the strain on them will be transferred directly to the wands. These tie-backs pass through a small hole in a leather washer sewn to the inner fabric. This arrangement usually provides enough friction to hold the liner back out of the way at any position desired. If wands are not used, the liner tie-backs can be installed at every outside guy line point. (See Fig. 2, Plate VIII, p. 100.)

FLOORS

Tent floors, especially when they are intended for use in wet weather and on snow, should be of a coated fabric. The floor of course takes a lot of hard wear. Using a coated fabric durable enough to remain completely waterproof for the life of a good nylon tent would add a lot of unnecessary weight. The center of the floor is a very easy part of the tent to replace, the center being the part which receives the most wear. The center can be cut out to within 2" or 3" of the sides and a new piece, cut a little oversize, can be sewn in with two rows of stitching on a 1" overlap. Though it is necessary to have a floor that water won't soak through, a few small holes and worn spots in the coating will never be noticed. It should never be necessary to use a floor fabric heavier than 8 ounces and if it's not too much trouble to renew the floor more often a lot of weight can be saved through the use of a single coated fabric as light as 3 ounces per square yard. When a single coated fabric is used place the coating on the inside of the tent. This not only saves it from abrasion by rocks and dirt but also helps sleeping bags stay put. Nothing is more annoying than a slippery nylon bag on a slippery nylon floor that slants slightly in one direction. It can make enemies out of the best of friends as they spend the night slipping together into one corner of the tent.

In view of the serious consequences of a fouled zipper on a high altitude tent only large zippers should be used and these kept to a minimum. Some people consider that a wide cover flap over the zipper is an advantage in that it helps prevent snow from being blown through the zipper, and in case of zipper failure it can be snapped or pinned shut. However the flap itself is a source of possible fouling and we personally install zippers in the clear with nothing covering them. Size 5 or 7 zippers should be used, except possibly in the light weight liner of a double walled tent or on a mosquito netting closure where size 3 can be used. Size 5 coil nylon zippers are also appropriate.

PEG LOOPS

The peg loops are points of considerable strain on a tent. These should be made of nylon where possible. On light weight tents not used in winter storms a good replaceable peg loop can be made by tying a 4″ loop of nylon cord and inserting it through a no. 1 grommet from inside. The knot keeps it from coming through and the loop is easily replaced when worn. A heavy hem, strip of webbing, or other strong reinforcing should be sewn around the tent floor to take the grommets.

For a more durable loop nylon webbing should be used. It is sewn to the floor which is first reinforced with a strong patch. This construction is durable enough to last for years, unless the pegs become frozen in and the loops have to be cut. Methods of sewing peg loops to corners or along the straight are shown in Fig. 8, Plate VIII, p. 100. Since the peg loops are usually the primary means of holding the tent in position against all the elements, care must be taken to distribute the strain over a large area of the floor by using reinforcing patches and very careful stitching so that no one stitch is out of line to take up the strain before the other stitches, thus starting a rip in the fabric. (See Fig. 3, Plate VIII, p. 100.)

ACCESSORIES

We have mentioned accessories for tents such as poles, wands, and pegs. They are extremely important to the backpacker. Since we are interested in light weight equipment only aluminum or magnesium poles will be described. It should be pointed out that when camping is done in timber it is often possible to rig some type of suspension from the trees so that poles should not be considered as essential items of equipment. Two pairs of skis and poles will pitch a small tent quite satisfactorily. Happily, commercial sizes of aluminum tubing are very adaptable to several types of poles. The ends for the poles will depend upon the type of tent they are to be used with. The major problem to be solved is how to make the pole sections short enough to be carried in the pack. For small tents 6061-T6 aluminum tubing, ⅝″ outside diameter with .028″ wall thickness, makes a fine light pole with ample strength in lengths up to 5½ or 6 feet. For joints, anything ⁹⁄₁₆″ outside diameter will make an easy slip fit inside the tubing. Four inches of tubing with 1¾″ permanently riveted on another length of tubing will leave 2¼″ protruding to form the joint. One of the best materials for the joint is light walled brass tubing. An aluminum to aluminum sliding joint is easily scored and can freeze together so it can't be taken apart. The hard brass slides easily on the aluminum. If these particular sizes of tubing are not available others can be used as long as the outside diameter of the joint material is .007″ to .010″ less than the inside diameter of the pole material. The joints, and whatever end fixtures are devised, can be held in position by drilling through the tubing and joint with a small drill. A small nail is inserted, cut off flush, and peened over.

For larger tents a telescoping sectioned pole can be made as easily as the sectioned pole. The following sizes of aluminum tubing will all fit into one another for an easy slip joint: ¾″, ⅞″, 1″, 1⅛″, 1¼″. All these sizes are 6061-T6, .058″ wall aluminum tubing. Poles made of such telescoping sections are also easily made adjustable. The sections must slip into one another at least 4″. About 4″ from the top end of the outside pole at each joint, drill a ⅛″ hole through both sides of the tubing. Three or four holes are drilled an inch apart below the first hole. A nail, a bit smaller than these holes, with the point cut off, will slip through these holes supporting the upper section of the joint. Each section adjusts about 3 or 4 inches. (See Fig. 4, Plate VIII, p. 100.)

The smallest diameter tubing is used for the top section and each section graduated one size larger down the pole. A 2-foot length is about the maximum convenient for backpacking, but they should be as long as possible since the more joints there are, the more wobble there is in the pole. To prevent their loss the pins for each joint can be tied on a long cord which will reach from joint to joint on the pole. A small bit of rubber can be pierced and pushed on the end of each pin when it is in position on the pole to prevent snags and scratches.

Telescoping poles should never be carried all telescoped together since the smallest piece of dirt or a slight dent or bend will leave a nice compact bundle of pole sections that can't be separated. When they are packed each section should be placed in the section *two* sizes larger. This will make two bundles instead of one but there will be no danger of their sticking together.

Spreader wands for a tent can be of any light flexible material. Since these have only to hold the fabric out and stiffen it against the wind they can be very light and thin. They should be sectional and the sections should be the same length as the tent poles so they will pack together nicely.

Very small aluminum tubing, less than $\frac{1}{4}''$ in diameter, will make an acceptable wand. Joints and the angle piece that form the top of the arch can be made of brass rod. This will probably have to be turned down to the proper diameter in a lathe or a drill, using a file, as the various diameters in the smaller sizes of aluminum tubing do not fit together as conveniently as the larger sizes used for poles.

One of the better wand materials is fiber glass such as fishing rods are made of. An easy way to get a first class wand is to buy two very cheap fiber glass fishing rods and cut the sections down to the proper size. If a one-piece rod is cheapest it can be cut into sections and regular fishing rod ferrules used to join them. Some supply houses can furnish the bare fiber glass blanks for fishing rods at considerably less cost than the completed rods. A thin strip split out of a piece of bamboo also makes a fair wand if it is large enough to take fishing rod ferrules to hold the sections together. The fixture holding the wands together at the top should be bent at a greater angle than the angle of the tent walls and it should be fastened securely to the ridge of the tent to prevent its loss and to keep the ridge from sagging.

Pegs are the last items of tent equipment to be considered. If the tent is to stay below timberline and if time is not at a premium, there is no reason to carry any pegs since they can be cut from small sticks on the spot. Considerable time in setting up camp can be saved if at least the key pegs are carried. A good peg for dirt can be made from $\frac{5}{8}''$ to $\frac{3}{4}''$ diameter tubing with one end cut square and the other at a long angle. A notch can be cut to retain the tent peg loop. This will hold nicely in fairly soft ground and can be driven in relatively hard ground too. For frozen or rocky ground nothing works quite as easily as a length of $\frac{1}{4}''$ or $\frac{3}{16}''$ steel rod with a loop on one end and a sharp point on the other. If this is to be driven in very hard ground it is a good idea to have the top loop welded shut so it won't flatten when pounded. Another method is to use a straight piece of rod with a washer welded near the top to hold the tent peg loop.

For use on soft snow or sand a peg with much more area is needed since the ground offers very little resistance. This kind of peg is best made by a tinsmith from .051″ or .040″ thick 2024-T3 aluminum sheet. The blank can be cut on a squaring shears and the angles then bent in a brake. Care should be taken that the bends are on a large radius (at least ⅛″) as a sharp bend will cause the hard aluminum to crack. If these stakes are driven in the ground at an angle nothing is needed at the top to hold the peg loop. However, it is a good idea to drill a large hole near the top, about ½″ in diameter. This hole can be used to tie down the tent peg loop if the stake can't be driven at enough of an angle. If the tent is pitched on snow it is very convenient to have the hole there to hook the ice ax or ski pole point through in order to break out the frozen stakes. (See Fig. 5, Plate VIII, p. 100.)

There are various other convenient tent accessories as shown in Figs. 6 and 7, Plate VIII, p. 100.

TENT LAYOUT

Tents are laid out as a series of triangles for convenience. As elementary geometry shows, given the length of three sides, only a specific triangle can result. A figure with more than three sides can take any shape unless one or more of the angles is known. However, a figure with more than three sides can be laid out as several adjoining triangles.

To lay out a triangle mark off the length of one of the sides as a baseline. The lengths of the other two sides are measured off on two straight edges. One end of each is made to touch each end of the baseline; the other two measured lengths meet at the apex of the triangle. Another method for measuring off a triangle is to use a wire or a piece of fishline (not string—too stretchy) in the same way a compass is used in grade school to construct triangles.

TENT FABRICS

Suitable fabric for specific tents depends on many factors. Unless very rainy weather in a fairly warm climate is to be encountered, coated fabrics should be avoided due to condensation. A good tightly woven 5½ ounce cotton fabric with a water repellent finish will shed water almost as efficiently as a coated fabric, especially if the pitch is steep and the tent large enough to prevent the occupants from rubbing against the inside.

The cotton also has the advantage of being inexpensive and is highly recommended as a "first" project or a pilot model of a new design. Cotton should never be left rolled up damp or it will mildew.

For the very lightest weight and greatest durability nylon is the fabric. But nylon does not readily absorb moisture and therefore deposits any condensation on the occupants in a most disagreeable manner.

To improve the condensation vs. water repellency problem in small tents, a double wall can be used with an outer rain fly of coated nylon. Total weight of both tent and liner or fly can be less than 4 ounces with greater durability for the main tent than if it is made of 5½ ounce cotton.

DESIGN ELEMENTS IN TENTS

There are some elements of design common to all tents. These are mainly concerned with the distribution of strain from the points at which it is applied to a wide enough area so that the relatively fragile fabric can accept it without tearing. In the case of any tent that is held up with one pole, the peak of the tent where the pole supports it must withstand all of the strain imposed by the weight of the fabric, the pull of the guy lines, and the wind or snow load. Needless to say this can mount up considerably and for this reason the peak should be well reinforced. In commercial tents of this type it is customary to hand sew a ring in the top with a hole for the spike in the top of the pole. This introduces a point of possible failure. A better way to meet the situation is to design the top of the pole as a truncated conical section without spike. The top of the tent can then be sewn completely closed with a small piece of soft leather in the tip of the peak to take the abrasion of the pole top. This makes a very strong weatherproof peak.

Tent walls often have attachments for guy lines to pull the sag out. An ordinary loop of web sewn directly to the fabric will very shortly rip out. The spot should be reinforced by a circular patch sewn to the tent fabric inside. This spreads the strain from a single point to a large circle to the single layer of fabric.

Another method of distributing this strain is to include in either a horizontal or a vertical seam a triangular flap of fabric with a grommet or web loop for the guy line at its apex and the base sewn into the seam. The weave of the fabric should be parallel to the base. This puts the two edges on a bias cut and allows them to stretch slightly so that the greatest strain is transferred to the tent at the center of the flap and gradually tapers off toward the ends. It is wise to plan to have the seams in the tent walls come at the right place to receive such pull out flaps.

A well designed and economical use of fabric sometimes necessitates piecing. The question of piecing the tent with vertical or horizontal seams can depend upon the stresses encountered, since the thickness and rows of stitching of a felled seam can be used as extra strong points to accept lines of stress from peg loops, guy lines, and poles. Another point to be considered in deciding how to piece the widths of fabric together is the water shedding abilities of the seams. Water will tend to run down vertical seams and may start to soak through near the bottom. Horizontal seams, properly felled so they lap like a shingle roof (felled *up* on the inside), will shed all the water collected on the fabric above. If these seams are always placed as high on the tent as possible a relatively small amount of water will pass over any one spot in the seam. If any trouble is encountered with seams leaking, they will have to be treated with a water repellent after the tent is constructed.

All tents contain points and lines of concentrated stress and after a certain length of time the fabric will stretch and reach its elastic limit along these lines and points and finally tear. To prevent this such points and lines are reinforced. Theoretically the reinforcing should have the same or a lower elasticity than the fabric and a higher strength. This insures that the reinforcing really accepts the load before the fabric and that it is strong enough to hold it without tearing. Of course, the fabric can be reinforced with another piece of itself which, if sewn on very smoothly so the two layers accept equal portions of the strain, will double the strength at that point.

In the case of point stresses, such as the peg loops, guy line attachments, and ridge peaks where the tent is held up by its poles, the reinforced area should extend back quite a distance from the actual point of stress so as to distribute this stress over a wide area before it is passed on to the single layer of fabric. In the case of a pyramidal tent where the entire weight is borne on one pole by the peak of the tent, you may wish to use a double thickness a foot from the peak, three thicknesses at the top six inches, and even four thicknesses the top two inches. This reinforcing gradually dissipates the strain from the point of the peak to a line about 4 feet long, where it is finally passed on to the single layer of fabric.

Stress lines, such as may exist between two guy lines at the ends of a ridge or between the top of a pole at a tent peak and the pegs holding it out, can be reinforced with light tape (it must not be stretchy), or, in light tents, a felled seam can be used along this line, thus helping the stress line accept considerably more strain than the bare fabric would take.

Any time something has to be sewn to the tent, such as a sleeve for an end pole or a pull out flap that can't be included in a seam, a tape should first be sewn to the inside along this line of strain, or the piece in question should be sewn on along the center of a felled seam, never to the bare fabric without reinforcing.

To make a tent that pitches smoothly and tightly without wrinkles is an accomplishment that not only adds to the beauty of the tent but also adds practical value in that there are no wrinkles to catch and hold snow and rain or, more seriously, to indicate localized strain. To help accomplish this, seams should be sewn without shirring and everything should be carefully cut to come out the proper length along joining seams, so no tucks have to be made for adjustment. The trick is to make every inch accept its share of the strain and no more.

Any line stretched between any two points, not directly above one another, will tend to sag from its own weight. All tent ridges hang in a slight curve and the fabric sags. To attempt to combat this by stretching the ridges very tightly puts an enormous strain on the tent. An easier solution is to design a little sag into these ridges. The "designed-in" sag eliminates the extra fabric that made the wrinkles and the wall remains flat and true. The amount of curve for these ridges is about ¼" per foot of ridge (a 6-foot ridge dips about 1½" in the middle). The curve can be laid out with a flexible strip of wood or metal—smoothly connecting the three points of ridge ends and the center point. (See Fig. 8, Plate VIII, p. 100.)

With practice on an inexpensive material the novice or the man with a new idea should be able to come up with a superior tent based on these facts.

MOUNTAIN TENT

LIST OF MATERIALS
Tent fabric—8 yards of 42″ or 8½ yards of 39″
Floor fabric—3 yards of 44″ or 3½ yards of 38″
¾″ Tape—6 feet
¾″ Webbing—5 feet
Grommets—6
Zippers—two 51″, open one end
    The above will make the basic tent with one zipper door. For optional extras and materials required, see below.

Options:
Rain fly—this requires 7 yards of the lightest possible water repellent or coated fabric about 40″ wide and includes double ends and side walls 9″ or more up on the inside of the tent. The edges are bound with 15 feet of ¾″ tape.
Storm sleeve door and vent—this requires 1½ yards more tent fabric and 9 feet of lace.
Cooking hole in floor—requires two 18″ zippers.
Aluminum poles—requires 204″ of ⅝″ diameter aluminum tubing.

INSTRUCTIONS
1. Read "Patterns and Sewing" to familiarize yourself with the operations and terms used.
2. Piece and cut two canopy parts no. 1. The lower piece of the wall is the full fabric width and the upper part is pieced. It is helpful to mark out the exact shape on the floor in chalk, place the fabric over it, and cut to shape. The two main lower wall parts are cut from the fabric, nesting the angles, then the two end parts no. 2 are cut also nesting the angles. The piecing on the ends no. 2 is also done at the top. After cutting these 4 main parts, two long strips of sufficient width to more than piece out the canopy parts are cut a little extra long. These are sewn with a finished felled seam to the top edges of the lower canopy parts. Fell the seam up on the inside. Lay the full canopy blank over the accurate outline on the floor, stretching the piecing seam and tacking to the floor if necessary. Trim the pieced section to exact shape. Use the same method for the other canopy and the two ends. The rest of the pieces are cut as needed.
3. Mark inside the canopy parts for the pull-outs and sew a length of tape on top of this line plus 1″ added to each end. Sew both edges of the tape. Cut out two pull out parts no. 3 with the goods parallel to the

long side of the material. Hem the two short sides with a ¾" plain hem and set a grommet backed by a leather washer in the point of the two hems. Using a top stitched seam, but folded over once more so there are no raw edges, sew the long edge of the pull out flaps to the outside of the canopy. Sew right between the two lines of stitching for the backing tape. Stitch back and forth at each end several times.

4. Cut 4 peak reinforcing patches from scraps about 6" long on a side. Sew these with a top stitched seam up into the top corners of the canopy parts, on the inside.

5. Join the ridges of the 2 canopy parts with a finished felled seam including the peak reinforcing patches. The patches should lie flat and smooth so they will accept the strain with the tent fabric. It is useful to include a few little loops of lace when felling the ridge as they are handy to use as hangers inside the tent.

6. Optional—If the tent is to be used in snow or with a rain fly the lower inside walls should be faced with a strip of the lightest coated fabric about 9" high. Sew the top edge of this with a top stitched seam across the canopy part inside. If a single coated fabric is used place the coating against the tent fabric. Do the same for the two ends.

7. Assemble the zipper door by sewing the zippers up the two side edges of one end part no. 2. Sew them so the zipper tape is even with the fabric edge for the first stitching and then roll the surplus fabric, or trim it off and top stitch with the second seam. See cross section detail Fig. 1, p. 113. The ends of the zipper metal should be ½" short of the edges of the original end part. Cut vent part no. 4 and hem the bottom edge around a piece of ¾" web. Stitch several times through the web. Sew this roughly over the peak of the zippers so the web bows out. The measured length of each side from zipper bottom to top corner of vent part should be 50" to 51".

8. Cut the top off the other end part so its side edges are 50" to 51" long. The flat top of the end is about 1" wide.
Optional—A door may be installed in the other end too. For use in warm weather another full opening zipper door can be made as in step no. 7. For high altitude or winter use, a storm sleeve can be installed. Simply cut a round or pear shaped hole in the end and mark in 6 equally spaced places around its edge. The sleeve should be a piece long enough to go around the hole, and should be marked to match the hole marks. The width of the sleeve piece should be 7" longer than the maximum radius of the hole (farthest out point to the center). Join the ends of the sleeve together to form a tube and sew the marked edge around the hole making the key marks match and at each key mark include one 9" length of lace on the outside and one on the inside.

These are used to tie the sleeve back or join two tents by their sleeves. Use a finished hem seam. A plain hem 1″ wide is sewn around the outer edge of the sleeve with a leather grommet at the top. Thread in a drawstring. A 5″ diameter sleeve vent can be installed the same way in the peak.

9. Optional—The tent may be pitched by tying the peaks between two trees but if above timberline, "A" poles at each end are recommended. These can be of ⅝″ diameter aluminum tubing, 51″ long, with a spike at the bottom and an eye or fork for the guy line at the top. Stout fiber glass fishing rod sections with ferrule joints make good poles too. Poles will require sleeves in the end seams of the tent for best results. These sleeves are 4 strips of fabric, cut 6″ x 36″ with the two ends hemmed. They are folded into long tubes and their edges pinned to the 4 end edges of the canopy parts so they will be included in the end seams when the ends are sewn to the canopy.

10. To sew the ends in, start at a bottom corner and use a finished felled seam, felled toward the canopy. Pin the seams first to be sure the peak will come out at the ridge because the ends are cut on the bias and will stretch if not controlled. Sew with the canopy on top and the end underneath. In the case of the zipper end, the edge of the zipper tape is ¼″ back from the rough edge of the canopy. Before starting, cut two 12″ lengths of web and include these at the peaks so 2″ tails extend inside and a 4″ long loop extends outside. The tails are well anchored to the ridge when felling this seam. See detail, Fig. 2, p. 113.

11. Cut and piece the floor part no. 5 to size. Sew reinforcing patches across each corner.

12. Optional—If a cooking hole is desired, install two 18″ zippers to meet at the point of an equilateral triangle.

13. Optional—If snow flaps are desired, cut enough strips about 9″ wide of light weight and preferably coated material to go along each side of the tent, 4″ short of each corner. Hem these on 3 sides and pin along the floor edges so they will be included in the seams.

14. Sew the floor into the tent with a finished felled seam, felled toward the floor. Pin in position first and if the floor is too big trim to match the tent sides.

15. Sew 9″ lengths of ¾″ web, preferably nylon, into the corners for peg loops. See Fig. 3. Hand sew with heavy nylon thread or fishline. If poles are to be used, set a grommet in one side of the peg loops, very close to the tent to take the spike of the pole.

16. Optional—A rain fly is made quite simply by cutting two panels as indicated for part no. 6 from the very lightest coated or repellent fabric. The long edges have tape sewn to them with a grommet or loop

in the center for a guy line. The ends are sewn on top of the end seams of the tent with a top stitched seam. This could be included when sewing the ends into the canopy but it is complicated for the beginner to keep track of all the layers.

Mountain Tent

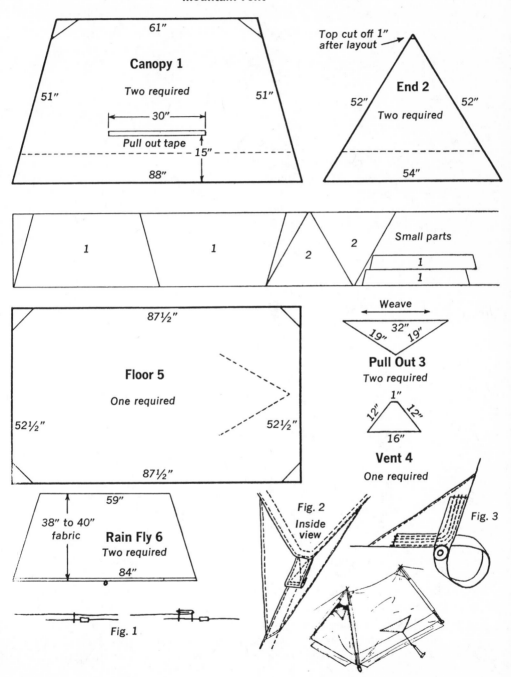

Canopy 1

Two required

61"

51"   51"

30"

Pull out tape

15"

88"

End 2

Two required

Top cut off 1" after layout

52"   52"

54"

1   1   2   2   Small parts

1

1

Floor 5

One required

87½"

52½"   52½"

87½"

Weave

Pull Out 3

Two required

19"   32"   19"

Vent 4

One required

1"

12"   12"

16"

Rain Fly 6

Two required

59"

38" to 40" fabric

84"

Fig. 1

Fig. 2
Inside view

Fig. 3

CHAPTER VII CLOTHING

In hiking, climbing, and camping, clothing assumes an importance we almost forget during the course of our centrally heated, aircooled, automobile-run lives. The torture of a large blister on a heel or the misery of improper clothing in a sudden snow or rain squall in the high country has to be lived through only once before attention to proper clothing becomes second nature.

GENERAL CLOTHING

A good wool shirt is a must for any outfit even in summer when it can act as a jacket, sweater, and windbreaker. Pure wool, or one of the woolly synthetics such as Orlon, is best. The fuzzy type of wool or synthetic fabric makes the warmest shirt when worn under a windbreaker, but is not itself very windproof. Therefore its usefulness as a windbreaker is limited. Wool kersey and doeskin have a heavily felted surface making them more wind resistant but they will not have the insulating qualities of the fuzzy fabric. The end use will determine what fabric is to be used, but for wind breaking or warmth the fabric should be 14 ounce or heavier. This weight is expressed in ounces per running yard of 60" wide material.

A regular dressmaking shirt pattern in the proper size and of the general cut desired makes the best pattern for a wool shirt. A sport shirt pattern is more satisfactory than a dress shirt pattern. There should be fullness across the back to allow for plenty of arm freedom and the sleeves should be cut almost straight out from the body. Changes can be made easily in this pattern to allow for individual tastes in details. For instance, the shirt tails will probably be eliminated in favor of a square cut so the shirt can be worn outside the pants like a jacket on occasion. The slit at the cuff can be eliminated and an adjustable snap strap cuff added for versatility. (See Fig. 1, Plate IX, p. 115.) Pockets can be installed to suit individual preferences and elbow patches for long wear can be added.

One change which makes a very versatile jacket shirt is eliminating the collar and substituting a regular parka hood. The parka hood pattern at the end of this chapter is very suitable. This hood will turn with your

PLATE IX

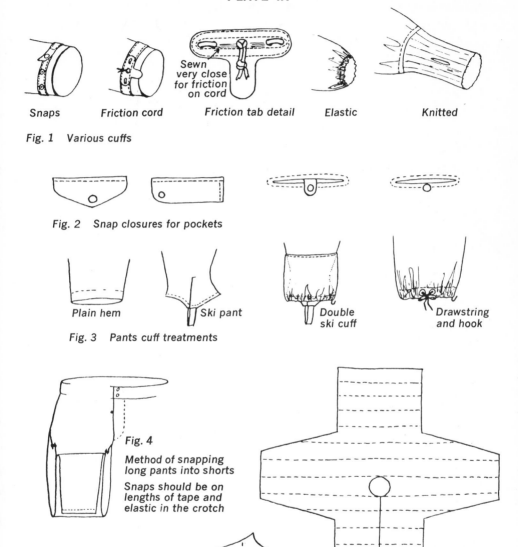

Snaps   Friction cord   Friction tab detail   Elastic   Knitted

Sewn very close for friction on cord

Fig. 1   Various cuffs

Fig. 2   Snap closures for pockets

Plain hem   Ski pant   Double ski cuff   Drawstring and hook

Fig. 3   Pants cuff treatments

Fig. 4

Method of snapping long pants into shorts

Snaps should be on lengths of tape and elastic in the crotch

Fig. 5   Simplified layout for down filled jacket and pants

head—many cowl types do not. The neck opening of the shirt pattern should be cut to match the shape of that in the parka so that it will take the hood. Both old and new neck holes should start at the same point at the back of the neck, but the hole for the hood will of course come way down in front. There is nothing quite so handy as having a nice warm woolen hood to keep the wind off the neck or to use as a warm lining for the light weight wind parka hood when necessary. Under a rain hat, for instance, this hood absolutely prevents those stray trickles finding their way down the back of the neck.

Climbing and hiking pants require a fabric entirely different from that used for shirts. They take much more wear and the fabric must be more abrasion resistant. The fabric should be hard surfaced, such as whipcord or twill, so it will wear well and won't tend to pick up snow as the fuzzy fabrics will. Wool and the wool-like synthetics are good for these pants too, even in summer, especially in rain. Nothing is quite so clammy as a pair of wet jeans unless the air is very warm. However, cotton jean material, or uniform twill, is a good inexpensive summer pants fabric. Since strength and durability are very important in pants fabrics a very high percentage of nylon, Dacron, or Orlon blends can be used. Some of the pure wool-like synthetics are much stronger than wool, especially when wet, and still have the performance of wool under most conditions, e.g., they feel warm when wet. As with the wool shirt pattern, it is convenient to get a commercial sport slack pattern to begin the project. Except for the general cut of the pants and the fly details, the commercial pattern will probably be abandoned in favor of one's own innovations.

The waistband should be wide and sturdy. A double thickness of the same pants fabric is very good. This should be cut 2″ deep so as to accommodate the widest belts. Sturdy belt loops, one on each hip and two in front, with a wide tunnel across the back, will support the pants comfortably without sagging no matter how much junk is in the pockets.

Pockets are more of a problem than at first appears. Ordinary pockets as shown on a slacks pattern might do for some hiking pants. These should be made considerably larger, down to full fingertip length (but no longer), and of an extra durable fabric such as nylon, or at least of the same fabric as the pants.

For rough going, or long trips away from civilization, it is a good idea to have one or all of the pockets made with some kind of closure so valuables (including compass and matches) won't be lost should a dunking in a creek or some other mishap take place—and they will take place! Zippers make a fine positive closure and are easy to put in. They can be hard on hands, especially cold chapped hands, but several things can be done to alleviate the scratching. First, use coil nylon zippers. Second, use 8″ zippers. This allows the pockets to open wide. In addition to the zipper pockets, which can be difficult to get into, you can make a large cargo pocket behind it. This can open at the top or have a flap overlap with its ends sewn down. This allows easy access to often needed items but prevents their dumping out if you end up upside down.

The other method of closing pockets is with a button or snap down flap. The flaps are made of two layers of fabric stitched around and turned inside out. For hip pockets a simple button or snap across the center of the opening keeps large objects from slipping out. (See Fig. 2, Plate IX, p. 115.)

The placement of pockets is left a good deal to personal taste. However, if much weight is to be carried in the pockets (anything heavier than a wallet and some change for instance) it is carried much more easily when it is suspended from the waist. This means to beware of those convenient looking pockets found on the outside leg of some old Army pants! These pockets can be loaded easily with a pound or two of junk which has to be lifted with the knee at every step. Quartermaster figures show that one pound carried here consumes as much energy as *three* pounds carried on the back and they have abandoned this design. Loose pockets hung inside the pants will tend to hang from the belt and let the knee and thigh slide up past them. If two side pockets and two hip pockets are made 8″ wide and fingertip length there will be an adequate amount of pocket space.

The seat of the pants takes a lot of wear even if hiking is the main idea. An added layer of fabric takes this wear. The extra layer over the seat also makes sitting on the cold ground more comfortable. The best way to add this thickness to the pants is to duplicate the shape of the pattern for the rear halves from about an inch or two below the waistband to about one inch below the crotch. These patches are sewn to the original pieces on the inside with a stitch across the top edge and bottom edge, before the whole pieces are sewn together to form pants. For winter use, the same thing can be done over the thigh to give warmth. These pieces should be extended down several inches below the knees and up to the crotch for added durability.

For climbers, rappel patches of soft chrome garment leather can be sewn under the thigh before the pants are assembled. These should be sewn on with heavy cotton thread as nylon will melt under the heat caused by the friction of the rope.

The bottoms of pants present several problems and several styles are usually necessary to satisfy all conditions. A simple hem 1″ wide will suffice for most general use. For skiing the lower leg is tapered to a snug fit around the ankle and socks and then flared out a little. A slit is made up the inseam so the foot can go through the narrow part. If this slit has to extend up past the boot top it should be backed by a fabric gusset to keep the snow out. Be careful not to have any hard or bulky seams in the area of the ankle bone as they become very uncomfortable after a few hours of skiing. This conventional ski pant bottom will not keep snow out of the boot top and this can mean cold wet socks and feet during extended trips. Separate anklets to keep snow out of boots will be described later, but the same idea can be sewn right into the pants—a double cuff, one going inside the boots and a second larger cuff sewn to the pants a couple of inches above the boot top with an elastic bottom that comes down well over the boot top. A large hook-eye hook can be sewn to the front edge to hook under the ski boot lace to keep the cuff down. This is a better method than a strap under the foot which soon wears out. (See Fig. 3, Plate IX, p. 115.)

For general mountaineering, where a hot walk in on forest trails can be followed by several hours climbing in snow, sometimes knee deep, the pants cuff problem is not so easy to solve. Shorts can be used for the hike in and ski pants for the climb, but this means the extra weight of two pairs of pants. Long pants can be fitted with snaps that allow the pants to be tucked up inside themselves forming knee length shorts. This leaves the long pants for the cooler high altitudes. If a drawstring is installed in the pants cuff, a hook sewn to the front, and the pants cut long enough, a fairly snowproof closure at the boot can be made by tying the drawstring up tight and hooking the hook under the boot lace to keep the pants down. This pattern which makes pants suitable for winter climbing can also be used for summer hiking. (See Fig. 4, Plate IX, p. 115.)

WIND PROTECTION

The outer layer of any outfit is the windproof layer. Although any type of jacket can be used for an outer garment as long as it is a tightly woven, water repellent fabric, a hood is highly recommended. A collar is of limited usefulness for protection from weather while a well designed hood can be worn to give varying degrees of protection. The design of the jacket itself in terms of pockets, drawstrings, zippers, and such is a matter of personal preference. A pullover design with a short zipper at the neck for ventilation is the most weatherproof. However, for warm weather, many people prefer the full length zipper that opens the front completely. The inside of either a short or full length zipper should be covered by a flap to keep the cold metal off the skin.

Generally speaking, the parka should carry no insulation itself. It should be of the lightest windproof material so that it can be worn over whatever amount of insulation weather conditions call for at the moment. If a very light material is used, a double layer over the chest and back can be used to give added wind protection and at the same time to form two large pockets between the layers. The pocket across the back is useful for carrying a surprising amount of gear when a pack is not carried. The large front pocket can be used for often needed items. If the parka is of the pullover type a kangaroo pocket is very convenient as its entire contents can be seen at a glance. Sometimes a large number of small pockets is more convenient. In this case patch pockets with zippers or flaps can be sewn all over the parka including the sleeves. For any parka it is a good idea to make the yoke over the shoulders and the center panel of the hood of double thickness since these two places receive the worst of it in a rain and soak through the quickest. Double layers give many times the repellency of a single layer.

The parka, being the windproof layer, must have a means of closing off the openings at wrists and waist. A drawstring at the waist will do the job here. If the parka has an extra long skirt a drawstring in the bottom may be desirable. Another method of handling the long skirt so it gives some protection in a wind is to snap it between the legs forming short pants of the bottom of the parka. Take care not to cut the skirt so long or narrow that it binds when a high step is taken.

The waist drawstring is a good place to use the drawstring clamp described under "Packs." This clamp eliminates fumbling with a tie drawstring under difficult conditions. If the parka has a full length zipper the ends of the drawstrings can be anchored at the zipper and the free ends brought through the drawhem at the center of the back. If a section of elastic is put in each side of the drawstring it can be tied to just the proper size and will be all adjusted whenever the parka is zipped up. This saves tying across the front every time the parka is zipped.

The closure of the parka cuffs can be handled several ways. Simplest of these methods is an elastic in the cuff hem. This gives windproof closure but has two serious drawbacks. One, it does not allow any ventilation. As pointed out under sleeping bags, ventilation is important in keeping moisture out of the insulation. Therefore the cuff closure should be adjustable. The other disadvantage is that those portions of the fabric that are bunched outward will wear out very quickly. Some sort of adjustable strap around the cuff with either a series of snaps or a piece of Velcro tape is a more practical arrangement. A variation on the elastic cuff is the addition of a knitted wristlet, though this does not provide ventilation either. It is possible to knit the wristlet so that there is a hole for the thumb allowing it to cover the fingers to the first joint. This feature often outweighs the lack of ventilation. It makes a fine cold weather rock climbing arrangement and also holds the cuffs down inside the mittens for a wind and snowproof joint. Separate ventilating zippers can be sewn in the sleeves just above the cuff.

A very useful cuff closure can be made with friction tabs and cords. A small tab is cut of soft leather and a drawhem with the tab on the inside of the wrist is sewn around the cuff about one inch from the edge. A spun nylon boot lace, or other rough cord, is threaded through the friction tab. This cuff is closed by pulling the knotted cord ends out along the hand, and opened by pulling the leather tab out away from the wrist. Friction of the tab on the cords holds it in any position. (See Fig. 1, Plate IX, p. 115.)

If you are going to do much rappelling when wearing the parka, especially if the parka is nylon, sew a leather rappel patch over one shoulder, with a flap extending up the neck, using cotton thread. The heat from the sliding rope will often melt nylon fabric and in any case causes undue wear.

The parka should be cut full enough to be loose over the maximum amount of insulation to be worn—loose even in a position with the arms extended ahead and up in an exaggerated reach. Any binding in the layers of garments will make cold spots. If ventilating clothing is not worn under the layers, the looser the garments the better. If a down jacket is worn and it has the type of sleeve that allows withdrawing the arms completely inside the jacket, then the outer parka must be cut to match it or the withdrawing feature is lost.

Every jacket tends to hike up at the waist when the person wearing it reaches above his head. The only way to eliminate this is to cut enough blouse above the waist to allow for the hike without raising the waist. There are no advantages to cutting the sleeves pointing up since the rise comes from the shoulders themselves and not just from the arms. If all sleeves are cut straight out, or slightly lower, there is sufficient allowance. Place the drawstring at the waist level when the arms are raised and this will eliminate the hiking up.

Wind protection for the pants need not be elaborate. The jacket is used much more often than pants due to the greater necessity of protecting the upper body from heat loss. Pants take more wear and tear so the more rugged pants are left outside as long as possible. However, there is no question that the addition of a windproof snow shedding layer to the pants will give a great deal of warmth when it is needed, and will keep the pants dry in the snow. The lightest nylon fabric can be used, cut to any pants pattern but with a few inches additional circumference to each leg. An elastic drawstring at the waist will enable the pants to be pulled down easily to get into the climbing pants pockets, and therefore no pockets or fly need be put in the wind pants to break their weather seal. The cuffs should have drawstrings so they can be left open for ventilation or be tapered to the ankle with zippers up the outside. A pair of pants such as this can be carried easily in a pocket and weighs only a few ounces.

INSULATION

The next consideration after a good quality shirt and pants and adequate wind protection is additional warmth, or the insulated layer. The amount of insulation required in cold weather depends not only on the temperature, but also on the degree of activity. Actually the thickness of the insulation required increases as the diameter of the object to be insulated decreases; thus more insulation is required for legs than body, more for arms than legs. However, in practice the opposite usually prevails since it is easier to put a greater amount on the body, with thinner insulation on the limbs to retain freedom of movement. This is not so detrimental as it may sound because the limbs act as radiators to control the heat of the body. If the body is kept very warm (this includes the head and face area which are very important sources of heat loss) it will send its excess heat to the hands and feet in an effort to get rid of it. In this way the extremities are kept warm even when insufficiently clothed. On the other hand, if the body becomes chilled one of its first defenses is to cut down on the circulation to the extremities in order that it may conserve its own heat. In this condition no amount of insulation on hands and feet will do any good.

Most of the time it is not possible to adjust the body insulation to match heat output exactly due to varying conditions of activity. One is either cold when inactive or overheated when working hard. Absolutely everything practical must be done to prevent sweating in cold weather as the moisture thus produced will find its way into the insulating layer and rob it of its insulating value. One great aid in this process is some kind of netting underwear which holds clothes away from the skin allowing the air to circulate more freely. This also allows the moisture to evaporate through ventilation from pants legs and cuffs out through the neck opening. Commercial net (Brynje) underwear is better than nothing though it tends to cut the air up into pockets rather than to encourage its free circulation. The old original shirt which was made of knotted fishnet served the purpose better, though it is rather uncomfortable under the load of a pack.

A shirt like the original knotted net type can be made by weaving ordinary cotton cord of a fairly large size into a regular net by methods covered in knot and craft books. Better yet, nylon braided cord can be used. The nylon is nonabsorbent and will thus get rid of the moisture better. Wide cloth or webbing straps can be used over the shoulders where the pack straps rub.

The basic idea of any of this underwear is to get rid of the moisture of perspiration before it can start to pass through the layers of clothing. If this moisture passes through the clothing it will eventually come into contact with a layer the temperature of which is below the dew or frost point. If this happens the moisture will either condense or freeze on that layer, causing much trouble.

As stated before, the amount of insulation furnished depends on the thickness of the insulation only, not on the particular material used, so long as it satisfies the condition of eliminating convection currents in the trapped air. There are no "miracle fibers" for insulating clothing, but as in sleeping bags, nothing surpasses waterfowl down. Not only will the lightest weight fill the greatest amount of space, but it will also compress the most for packing. Down makes a comfortable garment due to this compressibility because it will not allow binding under the arms and in those areas where bulk is uncomfortable. Just how much insulation to build into a down jacket depends on what its use will be. Ice fishing, for instance, requires more insulation than hiking or skiing. A table of the various thicknesses required for various degrees of activity is given below.

This should help in designing garments of the proper thickness for the conditions they will be used under. Since it is impossible to design for maximum thickness on all parts of the body some compromise must be made. The usual maximum practical thicknesses are 4" on the torso and 2" on the arms and legs.

It is important to remember that the garment must maintain this thickness in use to be of value. The differential cut of the fabric is even more important here than in the sleeping bag. For every inch of thickness the outside layer must be 7" greater in circumference than the inside layer. Over the shoulders, the differential cut must be vertical and although this extends down the arms there must be differential in both directions at the actual shoulder to allow for fullness when the arms are down at the sides.

Inches of Insulation Needed
According to Still Air Temperature and Activity

From Burton's *Man In A Cold Environment* using a practical insulation value for clothing of 4 clo/inch.° Thickness is measured from skin to outer garment layer.

Temperature	Sleeping	Light Work	Heavy Work
40°F	1.5"	.8"	.20"
20°F	2.0"	1.0"	.27"
0°F	2.5"	1.3"	.35"
−20°F	3.0"	1.6"	.40"
−40°F	3.5"	1.9"	.48"
−60°F	4.0"	2.1"	.52"

°One clo is the unit of thermal insulation which will maintain a resting-sitting man, whose metabolism is 50k cal. per square meter per hour, indefinitely comfortable in an environment of 21° Centigrade, relative humidity less than 50% and air movement of 20 feet per minute.

Differential at the elbow also helps. Wind pressure must also be considered and the compartments a little overstuffed with down so they don't flatten out in a strong wind.

The preceding description is of a jacket designed for maximum protection and should not be interpreted to mean that anything less is useless. Indeed, a plain quilted jacket of Dacron batting can give up to an inch of insulation and be ample for most uses, far surpassing the equivalent in sweaters and wool shirts when it comes to wearing ease and compactness in packing. With the clear understanding that the basic requirement of an insulating layer is maintaining a certain insulation thickness, one can readily decide which refinements to add to a simple jacket to make it give more and more insulation without increasing the weight of the materials used.

It is worth mentioning that a down filled hood is very very warm but almost impossible to hear through, even if thin spots are stitched over the ears. If a hooded wool shirt is used under a windproof parka hood, a down hood will probably never be needed. The impairment of hearing can be dangerous under some conditions.

There are two types of insulating jackets. One is exclusively insulation made to go underneath a windproof garment which also carries the pockets and other gadgets. The other type is actually an outer jacket with an insulating lining. The former can be made of the lightest nylon fabric. The second type should be made with an outside fabric sufficiently strong to wear well. Nothing over 5 ounce weight should be used, however, or it will have to be stuffed with extra insulation in order to push the heavy stiff fabric out to the required thickness. The inner fabric can be light weight and should be slippery so as not to bind on the clothes. A slippery outer fabric will greatly reduce the bulky binding feeling too, especially under the arms.

If you are making an outer wear jacket, you will probably want pockets. If the jacket is fingertip length there is usually a surplus of insulation below the waist anyway, so a couple of pockets stitched through both layers won't make much difference. A handy combination of hand warmer and snap flap pocket can be sewn on below the waist. Another combination is a couple of slash hand warmer pockets actually surrounded by down up on the chest, and two patch pockets, to hold gloves and such, below the waist. The collar should be full and puffy so it fits close to the neck and comes up under the ears. If you want a hood for extreme conditions it can be snapped on outside the base of this collar which forms a draftproof seal.

The cuffs of the insulating jacket can be left open if it is being worn under a windproof layer, or it should have some means of adjusting the cuffs and waist if it is the outer layer. Velcro tape and snaps or plain snaps should be used to close the jacket. A double zipper that opens from the bottom as well as the top is convenient, but more subject to malfunction.

Insulated pants require the same considerations as insulated jackets except that the crotch and inseam can be stitched through completely with little loss in efficiency. Pants are so warm that they can become unbearable as the day warms up so the pants should be made to pull on and off easily over the climbing boots. Suspenders should be avoided since the jacket must be removed to put them on. If the pants are snapped to the inside of the jacket they can be put on without removing the jacket. A rear "fly" of generous dimensions is a great convenience in down pants.

Insulating pants are of the same two types as the jackets—either a separate insulating layer worn under wind pants, or an outer garment. In the latter case they require pockets and rugged outer fabric. The resulting thickness of clothing can be determined by using the same tables applied to sleeping bag construction. A simple method of constructing both pants and jacket is illustrated in Fig. 5, Plate IX, p. 115. The pieces are constructed with differential cut, but the tubes are filled with down while the pieces are laid out flat, as shown. The inseams of the pants and jacket underarms are then stitched together.

HANDS

Hands come next on the insulation list. They are always difficult to insulate properly. One of the best provisions for keeping hands warm is a jacket that keeps the body so warm that the excess heat is sent to the extremities. For severe conditions, jacket sleeves with gussets from elbow to waist to allow the arms to be withdrawn inside the insulation next to the body are very practical. Once the hands are withdrawn inside such a jacket all sorts of things can be done in comfort, such as note taking and eating lunch, without ever exposing the hands to the cold. Of course, hands and arms must be used most of the time and they will eventually become cold, but they need never stay cold if they can be withdrawn inside the insulating jacket to warm up again.

The size of mitten needed to keep hands warm on an inactive man at $-60°F$ would be about as big as beer barrels. A reasonable amount of insulation can be provided by about 2" of down on the back of the hand and thumb like a boxing glove. When the fist is closed this almost surrounds the hand with insulation. At the same time the fingers can lie next to a thin leather palm so they can handle simple objects. If a third layer of insulation is added across the palm so the fingers have a choice of slipping between the two layers of insulation or lying next to the thin leather, the mitten will be warmer and more versatile.

The construction of a maximum protection-minimum bulk mitten is a complicated and difficult process. A mitten with only an insulated back will give a good deal of insulation and be easier to make. Using an ordinary ski mitten pattern, or an old mitten taken apart as a pattern, cut one regular back piece and a second back piece which is about one inch bigger all around. Assemble the mitten as directed but with the second back piece going outside of the regular back. Take tucks to make them come out even at the key points around the palm. The space between the double back can be filled with down through an opening left at the wrist. It will also be a good deal more convenient than the conventional arrangement of several layers of wool gloves or mitts inside a windproof shell. In order not to impair ventilation at the cuffs the mitten can be designed to go inside rather than outside as is usual with the gauntlet type.

It is a good idea to use a thin glove under insulating mittens because, although it adds little to the insulation since each finger is isolated, if the mitten is removed to allow greater dexterity for some operation, the glove remains to give a little protection to the bare skin. Air Force mechanic's rayon anti-contact gloves serve this purpose very well. It is possible to operate cameras and get things out of boxes and pockets with these gloves.

Many times the dexterity of a glove is required and a mitten is inconvenient. If the glove is kept very loose and the body kept good and warm to send a supply of blood to the hands these gloves can be used at surprisingly low temperatures. A loose fitting soft leather glove with a couple of pairs of knit wool liners that can be removed for drying or replacing makes a good outfit.

FEET

The next and last portion of the body which needs increased insulation at low temperatures is the feet. While this isn't a short course in shoe making, there are several methods of protecting the feet against the cold and wet. First, there is the nylon stretch ski pant fabric anklet that simply makes a snowproof and gravelproof closure around the boot top so snow doesn't get in to wet the socks. These require a hold down hook to go under the boot lace to keep them in position. A strap under the foot works better than the hook but wears out quickly, so should be replaceable by being tied to loops sewn to the anklet.

For work in deep wet snow in conjunction with rock climbing where the lug soles of the boot must not be covered, a gaiter or legging is in order. These can be made of any of the fabrics suitable for packs. The army leggings are a good pattern to follow but should be made tubular instead of being split. This prevents any gaping holes. The excess fabric is between the lacings. The whole legging is cut large enough to slip on over the boots.

Long snow climbs in very cold temperatures necessitate complete overboots. This boot encases the climbing boot and prevents snow and wet from ever reaching boot or socks.

A plain fabric overboot adds greatly to the warmth of the feet by keeping the feet dry, but this is also a very good place for the addition of a little insulation. A quarter inch of some closed cell foam rubber or plastic, such as Ensolite, incorporated in the overboot will protect the feet at extreme temperatures and still allow a well fitted climbing boot. The foam insulation should be encased between two layers of fabric so the boot can be slipped on easily. This insulation need only extend down to the edge of the sole and 10″ up the leg of the overboot. The overboot itself comes up just under the knee. The foam insulation may be slipped into a pocket in the overboot, making the boot lighter and more easily handled when the insulation is not needed. The pocket should be open around the bottom edge so the insulation can be inserted with the boot inside out. It will be held in place by the sole when the boot is right side out. The pocket should be sewn closed for a few inches around the heel and toe, but plenty of opening can be left along the sides to insert the piece of Ensolite. (See Fig. 1, Plate X, p. 127.) If hooks are used on one side of the lacing and grommets on the other, the lace can be left in the grommets and tied at the top permanently. The loop between each grommet can be pulled over a hook until the top is reached. There will be just enough give in the whole system to let the last loop slip over the last hook and pull itself up tight.

The sole of the overboot should be double thick fabric or a nonstretchy chrome leather. A 1½″ double fabric or chrome leather strip runs around the lower edge of the upper to take the wear from crampons.

The sole pattern of the overboot should be cut about ¾″ larger all around than the outline of the boot sole they are to be used with. The uppers must have a very stubby toe and large circumference to allow the boot to be slipped inside. The extra fabric is between the lacing so it gets pulled in snug to the leg when the boots are laced. The insulation itself is cut only to encircle the leg with nothing extra. This combination with a couple of pairs of heavy wool socks in a good boot will keep the feet warm at almost any temperature.

RAIN PROTECTION

Rain protection is necessary in any but a dry climate and for anything more than a one day trip. Most water repellent clothing will shed a shower

PLATE X

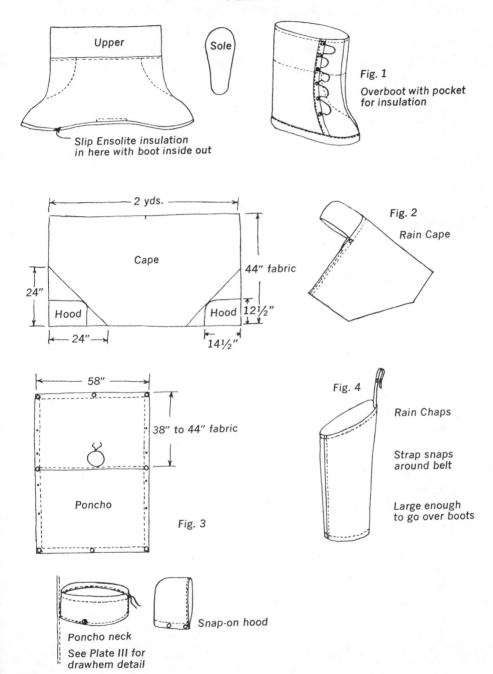

Upper

Sole

Slip Ensolite insulation in here with boot inside out

Fig. 1
Overboot with pocket for insulation

2 yds.

Cape

44" fabric

24"

Hood   Hood   12½"

24"   14½"

Fig. 2
Rain Cape

58"

Poncho

38" to 44" fabric

Fig. 3

Fig. 4

Rain Chaps

Strap snaps around belt

Large enough to go over boots

Poncho neck
See Plate III for drawhem detail

Snap-on hood

for a short time but eventually will soak through. If a wool shirt and a ventilating shirt are worn underneath the clothes a considerable amount of soaking can be tolerated. For protection against prolonged rain, something made of a waterproof fabric must be worn. Close fitting jackets and pants are generally unsuitable for backpacking because of the amount of condensed moisture they collect inside. This can make one just as wet as the rain outside. In some special cases such an outfit is satisfactory and a parka and pants of the same cut as the wind parka and pants can be made very simply from a single layer of a very light weight coated nylon fabric, or even of sheet plastic material. Seams can be sewn or cemented. If the seams are sewn they should be coated over with some sort of rubber cement to make them waterproof.

The best all-purpose rain protection is usually a poncho or rain cape that fits over the pack and all. There is a good deal of air circulation underneath a cape which is draped over a pack allowing the body moisture to be carried off. A hood is a great help too to keep the water from running down the neck. A rain cape is the lightest possible protection, generally being about fingertip length, and either snapping up the front, or in a pullover style with no sleeves. (See Fig. 2, Plate X, p. 127.)

A poncho is similar but rectangular with a hole in the center for the head. It folds over the shoulders and snaps down the sides with the arms coming out each side under the fold. The larger poncho can also be made to cover both the pack and the hiker down to the knees. One disadvantage is that its very largeness makes it difficult to control in the wind. In spite of its heavier weight its increased versatility makes it a good choice. Grommets set at the corners and centers of the sides make it a good ground cloth, or the snaps can be used to snap it into a tent floor. By alternating the snaps, male and female around the edge, two ponchos can be snapped together to make a rather large tarp or tent. When it is used as a ground cloth or tarp, once camp is set up it cannot be used as a personal rain garment.

Also, if the poncho is to be used as a tarp there must be a means of closing the neck hole securely. This can be done by using a sleeve higher than half the diameter of the hole. This sleeve is then closed with a drawstring. When using it as a poncho, a snap-on hood can be used with this closure. Since the neck protrudes from the forward part of the body, the neck hole of the poncho should be cut forward of the center line of the poncho. The neck opening should be advanced even a little more if the poncho is to be worn over a large pack, and the side snaps adjusted accordingly. (See Fig. 3, Plate X, p. 127.)

To keep the pants dry, not only from the water draining off the poncho or cape, but also long after the rain has stopped, in wet brush, a pair of chaps made of light weight coated nylon are well worth carrying. These slip over each leg and are very simply made by sewing a tube large enough to go over the boot easily and long enough to reach to the crotch on the inside and a few inches higher on the outside of the leg. A snap strap that goes up around the belt secures them, or they can be simply pinned to the pants. These can also be cheaply made from a length of plastic bag tubing. (See Fig. 4, Plate X, p. 127.)

PARKA

LIST OF MATERIALS

Fabric—4 yards 42″ or 39″, for 36″ fabric or larger sizes, add ¼ yard to ½ yard

Lace—8 feet

Zippers—two 8″ pocket zippers for double slash pockets if desired
one 11″ locking for neck if pullover style
one 34″ separating jacket style if jacket

Elastic—18″ for elastic cuffs if desired.

Dot Snappers—6 male and 2 female for snap strap cuffs if desired

INSTRUCTIONS

1. Read "Patterns and Sewing" to familiarize yourself with the operations and terms used.

2. Make up a paper pattern for the various pieces, including alterations for your individual size and desires. The pattern given is for a 36–40 with 33 sleeves although there is a good deal of leeway with a garment as loose fitting as this. The yoke and hood should fit well, so it is best to cut these pieces out of some scrap fabric, assemble roughly, and try on for fit. Sleeves should be long enough for a forward and upward reach. The waistline should be indicated on the pattern and it should hang free about 4″ below your waist so there is enough blouse to accommodate arms raised directly overhead. The skirt should not be longer than the top of the knees or it will bind if a big step is taken. Types and number of pockets should be considered. If a pullover style is preferred, a kangaroo pocket across the front (as in the sketch, page 134) is convenient. Simply install a single horizontal zipper about 12″ long instead of the two slash zippers shown on the pattern. By placing an extra zipper in the back outer layer under one arm you can make a pocket all the way across the back between the inner and outer layers.

3. Mark fabric from patterns and cut out. Be sure you cut one full size part no. 1 Front and part no. 2 Back, and one each down to the waist only. Cut two sleeves, part no. 3, two yokes, part no. 4, two hood side pieces, no. 5 (one right and one left if the fabric is not reversible), and two hood center pieces, part no. 6. Save the scraps for drawhems and cuff tapes.

4. If you are making a pullover style part no. 1 Front will be whole; if a jacket style, this part can be cut exactly down the center. In either case, cut the slits for whatever arrangement of pocket zippers is desired and install the zippers with cover flaps or bare.

5. Place the inner back and front pieces against inside of outer back and front pieces and pin in position. Treat these pairs as single pieces from now on.

6. Using an insertion seam, inset the back between the two yoke pieces. A couple of inverted box pleats in part no. 2 Back will make it come out even with the yoke. Pin this seam before sewing and stitch. Using the same method, insert the front between the yoke pieces. No pleats are needed.

7. The hood Side Pieces no. 5 are inserted between the two hood Center Pieces no. 6 with an insertion seam. Start at the front "A" and work over the head toward "B." Inserting the second side piece is more difficult since the entire hood is inside the center pieces but it can be done.

8. The hood is sewn into the neck hole in the body with a finished felled seam. Start at the back of the neck and work down each side, or pin in position first. The seam is felled toward the body and you can include a hang up loop at the back of the neck if desired.

9. If you want snap strap cuffs, cut two pieces 3" x 16" and fold down the center, then fold edges in to the center, making 4 thicknesses and no exposed edges. These ¾" wide straps are sewn across the cuffs, one facing right and one left, as indicated in detail Fig. 1.

10. Sew the sleeves into the arm holes of the assembled body. The edge of the sleeve with the cuff strap protruding is the rear edge of the sleeve. If no cuff straps are used the sleeves are the same either way. Use a finished felled seam and fell up toward the body so water will drain off the finished parka.

11. Sew up the sides of body and sleeves. Use a finished felled seam felled toward the back. Catch one end of the cuff tapes if used, but leave the long end free.

12. Sew a plain hem ½" wide around the bottom edge of the parka. If the parka is to be snapped between the legs, include a 4" tab of fabric as in step 9 in the center of the back. Set a snap in this and in the hem itself, front center.

13. Install the front zipper, either a short neck type for a pullover, or a full length one for jacket style. The top stops should be about ½" below the edge of the hood face hole. The bottom of the jacket zipper should not reach quite all the way to the bottom hem. If you have shortened the skirt so much that the zipper is too long, cut the zipper off at the top end and sew it right up to the edge of the hood. Then when facing the hood, the facing must be run out past the zipper teeth. This will form a top stop to prevent the slider from coming off. If the zipper is covered on the inside by a flap of fabric or piece of tape it will keep

the cold metal off the chin and help prevent clothing getting caught.

14. Install a facing drawhem around the face opening of the hood, as explained in "Patterns and Sewing." Thread in a lace drawstring and stitch the ends of the drawhem opening as tightly as possible around the lace, twisting the lace to make it smaller. This will provide sufficient friction to hold the adjustment without need for tying. Anchor the drawstring by a few stitches in the center to prevent its being pulled out accidentally.

15. If elastic cuffs are to be used, sew two elastic loops just snug but not tight on the wrist. Hem the cuffs over these loops with a ¾" plain hem. If snap straps are used, just hem the cuffs. Then set a female snap in the tag ends of the cuffs about 1" from the actual end. Set one male snap so the tag end just reaches it. Set another over as far as you will ever want the cuffs to be tightened, and set a third midway between these two.

16. Cut and piece a waist drawhem that will go all the way around the parka. Install inside, using the waist drawhem method as explained in "Patterns and Sewing." Cover rough edges of the inner back and front pieces at the same time. For pullover style, a leather grommet is sewn in front for the lace drawstrings to come out. For jacket style it is convenient to install the leather grommet in the center of the back. See instructions for this in the section—"Wind Protection" in this chapter.

Parka

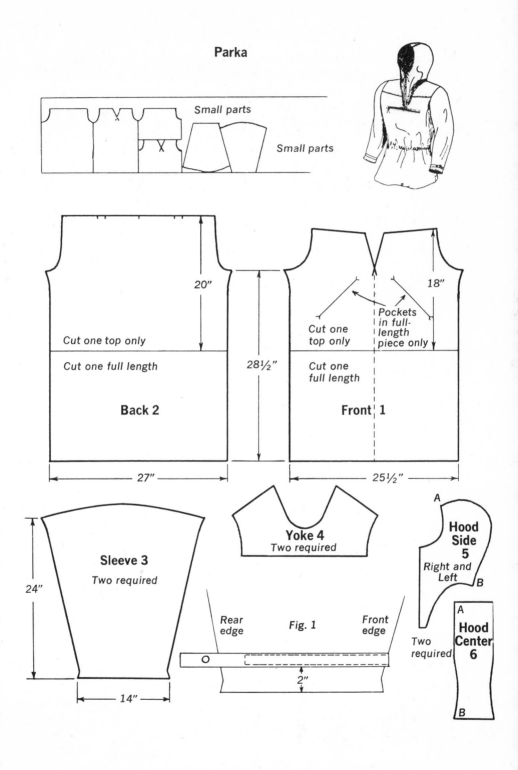

Small parts

Small parts

20"

Cut one top only

Cut one full length

Back 2

28½"

27"

18"

Cut one top only

Pockets in full-length piece only

Cut one full length

Front 1

25½"

Sleeve 3
Two required

24"

14"

Yoke 4
Two required

Rear edge

Fig. 1

Front edge

O

2"

A

Hood Side 5
Right and Left

B

Two required

A

Hood Center 6

B

Parka

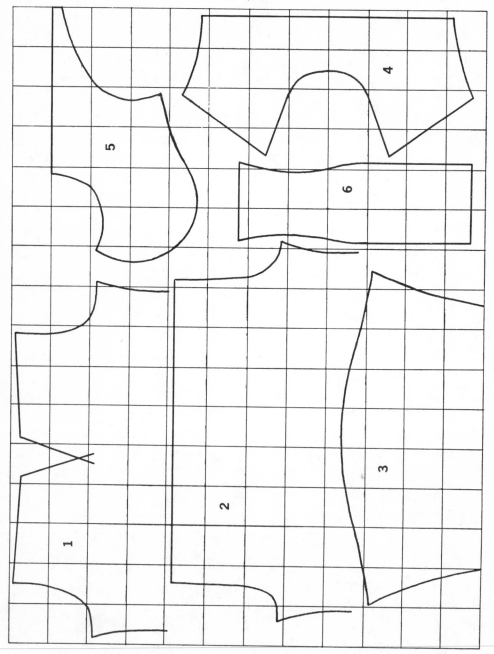

3" squares

DOWN SWEATER

Dimensions for several sizes are given for the down sweater because this garment fits more closely and changes in size must be scaled carefully for sleeve and collar fit. The down sweater was designed by Dale Johnson of Frostline, Broomfield, Colorado.

UNFINISHED DIMENSIONS

Back	Large (Man) X-Large (Lady)	Medium (Man) Large (Lady)	Small (Man) Medium (Lady)
Neck to bottom	33½	31½	29½
Armhole	13	12	11¼
Chest	26¾	25	23¼
Front			
Neck to bottom	33½	31½	29½
Width	13¾	13	12
Neck depth	5	5	4¾
Pocket			
Width	13⅝	12½	11½
Height	15	14¼	13¼
Cutout	5	5	5
(+ 1½″ offset)			
Collar			
Length	20⅛	19¾	19¼
Depth	4⅛	4	3⅝
Sleeve			
Shoulder to cuff	31	29	28
Width at armhole	24¼	23¼	21¾
Width at cuff	16¼	15	14¾

XL and XS sizes are proportional

Down Sweater

	X-Large (Man)	Large (Man) X-Large (Lady)	Medium (Man) Large (Lady)	Small (Man) Medium (Lady)	X-Small (Man) Small (Lady)
Down Total Ounces°	8½	8¼	7	6½	5½
Separating Zipper	26″	24″	22″	20″	18″

°Includes an additional ¼–½ ounce for spills and evening out distribution.

Fabric—approximately 6 yards of 36″–39″ or 5 yards of 45″ wide material for size medium; proportional amount for other sizes

Elastic—½″ wide flat; length to fit wrist dimensions + ½″ (or substitute cord for friction cuff)

Lace—¼″ nylon, 3″ long

Cording—10′ long

Dot Snappers—3 (if hood is to be added)

INSTRUCTIONS

1. Read "Patterns and Sewing" to familiarize yourself with the operations and terms used.

2. Make up a paper pattern for the various pieces in the size you plan to make, including obvious alterations. Pin together and try on for approximate fit. You will have an outside and a lining for each piece.

3. Mark fabric from patterns cut out, noting in the illustration the number required of each piece. Pockets and fronts will have a right and left. Mark these for identification. Sear edges of nylon (see page 41).

4. Fronts, backs, and sleeves have 4 small marks on each outside edge. Pockets have one mark on each side. These are guides for marking quilting lines. Mark quilting lines on one right and one left front, on one back, two sleeves (no right or left), and on one right and one left pocket. Use tailor's chalk or a white pencil, and with a yardstick mark from edge mark on one side to edge mark on other side, 4 lines on each piece, except for pockets, which have one. Make lines as fine as possible, but still visible. *Lined side will be right side of fabric.* Make sure lines across front exactly match at center front.

5. Make collar: Set 3 Dot Snaps in one collar piece if desired for hood

attachment. With snaps use small reinforcement squares inside collar. Match edge marks on two collar pieces; stitch together around curved edge. Turn right side out. Sew bottom closed with $\frac{1}{4}''$ seam allowance, except for 5" opening.

6. Fill collar with down, about $\frac{1}{4}$ ounce. Stitch opening closed.

7. Assemble outside and lining: Stitch outside fronts to back at shoulders, right (lined) sides together. Join lining fronts to back in the same way.

8. Cord the four front edges: Cut cording into four equal lengths. Fold front edges $\frac{3}{4}''$ (NOT LESS) around cording to wrong side. Stitch with zipper foot as close as possible to cording. Cut cording off $\frac{1}{2}''$ above bottom.

9. Pin 3" lacing in a loop to center of lining neckline for a hang loop.

10. Stitch around necklines of outside and lining to keep them from stretching (staystitch): Stitch around each neckline $\frac{3}{8}''$ from edge. Clip edge every inch, but do not cut stitches. Sear cuts.

11. Place lining and outside right sides together. Insert collar between them, raw edge along raw edge of neckline. Make sure that snaps on the outside of collar are against OUTSIDE (lined side) of sweater. Make collar ends even with cording. Stitch across, backstitching at each end. Make sure stitching is inside row of staystitching.

12. With sweater still wrong side out, pin backs together and fronts together so assembly lies flat. Match shoulder seams. Pin and stitch armholes together. Clip every inch on underarm curve, being careful not to cut stitches.

13. Turn right side out: Insert hand between bottoms of back; reach up over left shoulder between layers, grasp two left fronts, pull through. Repeat for right fronts.

14. Stitch side seams: Lay sweater right side out so all four layers are touching at sides. Fold lower corner of outside front up to expose lining front side edge. Pin lining front to lining back from armhole to bottom. Fold outside front to rear so its side edge meets outside back side edge; pin, making continuation of lining seam, with armhole seam crossing it in center. Make sure that ends of armhole seam match. Stitch from bottom edge of outside to bottom edge of lining. Repeat on other side.

15. Return sweater to right side out position. Fold fronts back to expose side seam. Pin outside and lining seams together. Stitch just outside seam stitching, starting $\frac{1}{2}''$ down from armhole seam. Stitch to bottom edge.

16. With right side out, topstitch edge of armhole $\frac{1}{8}''$ from edge. (Do not stitch shoulder seams together.)

17. Install zipper: A separating coil zipper may be stiff and hard to work

when new. Separate and join it several times before sewing to loosen up. Separate zipper. Place half with slide between corded edges of sweater's right front. Fold top of zipper tape back and tuck up into neckline as high as it will go. Pin zipper so corded edges just cover zipper teeth. Stitch with regular presser foot against cording to give about ¼" space between rows of stitching. If your regular presser foot is too wide to catch zipper tape when one edge is against cording, use zipper foot with its edge against cording. Start and end with backstitch. When you approach zipper slide, stop with needle down, raise presser foot, and push slide behind presser foot, so stitching does not bulge going around the slide.

18. Close zipper. Pin to corded edges of sweater's left front in the same manner. Be sure that neckline seams match. Unzip zipper and stitch as for right front.

19. Make two complete sleeves. Be sure quilting lines are on INSIDE. Stitch sleeve pieces together along sides and curved end. Leave wrist edge open. Clip every ½" in curved areas. Turn sleeve right side out, poke corners out against seam, and topstitch around seamed edges ⅛" from edge.

20. Make a left and a right pocket: Stitch around all edges of pocket except bottom. Be sure each pocket has a quilting line on inside at this step. Turn right side out, press seams. Topstitch diagonal edge ⅛" and ⅜" in from edge.

21. Down filling: Pin bottom closed in a line 2½" above edge. Leave 6" opening in bottom of each front and back. Pin shoulder seams together so down cannot shift from fronts to back.

22. Ounces of Down

	Each Front	Back	Each Sleeve	Each Pocket
X-Small	½	1½	1	¼
Small	¾	1¾	1¼	¼
Medium	¾	2	1¼	¼
Large	1	2¼	1½	¼
X-Large	1	2½	1½	¼

Fill each front, sleeve, pocket, and the back compartment with amount of down listed on the chart above. Stitch across bottoms ¼" from edge. Distribute down evenly in each piece. On sleeves and fronts, push a little more down into upper halves.

23. Quilting: Zip sweater together and check to be sure quilting lines match across zipper. Unzip, distribute down evenly in fronts and back, also in sleeves and pockets. Push plenty of down into both front and

back top compartments so shoulders will fill when pins are removed. It is possible to stitch quilting lines without pinning if you are very careful, but you may wish to pin across all lines from one front edge around sweater to other front edge. Be sure pins (or stitches) do not pucker or tuck lining underneath. The commonest problem in quilting is catching material underneath as you sew. Smooth very tightly with your hands to each side of the presser foot to avoid this. Look underneath as you proceed to check for puckers and tucks. On sweater, stitch second line from bottom first, bottom line next, then top two. Backstitch at each end of lines. On sleeves, pin and stitch third line from bottom first, top line next, then bottom two. Stitch line on pockets. Remove shoulder seam pins.

24. Sew pockets onto sweater: Pin pockets on fronts with tops along second quilting line from bottom of sweater, front edges along zipper stitching line, side edges along sweater side seams. Zip sweater closed. Check to see that tops of pockets line up. Stitch, starting with backstitch at top of pocket opening, across top of pocket, and down front edge to bottom. Stitch side edge, starting with backstitch at pocket opening, down side seam to bottom.

25. Hem sweater: Turn bottom edge of sweater, including pockets, up ¼", then ¾" to lining side. Be sure measurement is made on sweater front, not pocket. Check to be sure bottom edges of front and stitching line of hem are even at center front. Stitch.

26. Stitch sleeves together lengthwise: Make seam just inside topstitching.

27. Join sleeves to body: Fold sweater so lining side is out. Place one sleeve (no right or left) right side out in armhole. Pin sleeve to armhole, with pins in sleeve. Start by matching underarm seams, pin all around. Sleeve should fit exactly, but if it is slightly larger, ease fullness in around top half of armhole by pinning every ½" with a tiny amount of fullness between each pin. Stitch around armhole. Make seam just inside edgestitching of sleeve.

28. Sleeves may be finished by making a casing for elastic and inserting elastic, or you may use a pair of knit cuffs. Other good closures for ventilation are illustrated in Fig. 1, Plate IX, page 115. Measure correct sleeve length by putting sweater on, closing zipper, and extending arm to front at shoulder height. Mark sleeve end at wrist. To make elastic casing, turn sweater inside out, turn back sleeve to marked position. If turned-back cuff is longer than 1", stitch around 1" from fold, cut off excess and sear edge. Turn edge under ¼", then ¾". Stitch. Leave a 3" opening in hem. Measure wrist for elastic. Cut two pieces ¼" longer than wrist length. Use safety pin to thread one through each sleeve end. Pull elastic ends out, overlap ½", and stitch

together well. Push back into casing, try on for fit of wrist. If fit is right, stitch casing closed.

To install knit cuffs: Pin around sleeve at length mark. Unless the pins fall on stitching at bottom of sleeve, stitch around sleeve at marks. Cut off sleeve end ¼″ below stitching. Sear edge. Turn sleeve wrong side out. Mark into quarters with pins. Fold knit cuff in half, raw edges together. Mark raw edge into quarters, with pins on inside of cuff, pointing out. Insert cuff into sleeve end, raw edges back ¾″ from raw edge of sleeve. Stretch cuff to fit sleeve end. Pin around through sleeve often enough to hold cuff in place. Fold sleeve end to inside ¼″, then ½″, pin around over raw edge of cuff. Be sure edge of cuff fits against fold of sleeve end. Stitch cuff in place, ⅛″ from edge of sleeve fabric, stitching through folded over edge of sleeve, double layer of cuff and outside of sleeve in one stitching. Turn sleeve right side out. Cuff is now installed with no stitching showing on outside.

You may wish to make a snap-on hood. One is illustrated in Plate X, page 127. Make trial pattern from old sheet or scrap and check for fit to collar and head. A double center section will provide more water protection. You probably will not need down—too warm.

CARE AND USE INSTRUCTIONS

For best appearance and warmth, spin your sweater in a dryer at moderate heat (150°) for about 15 minutes before wearing it the first time. This will restore maximum thickness to the down, which has been compressed in construction. Protect zipper by having sweater zipped closed while in dryer.

Your down insulated garment may be either drycleaned or washed. Washing does not harm the down. HAND wash your sweater in warm, not hot, water using a mild detergent. DO NOT use enzyme-type cleaning agents. Scrub any especially dirty areas with a brush. Use WARM, not hot, setting on dryer and dry thoroughly before use—four or five times more drying time than for other types of garments.

After use, it is a good idea to spin jacket in dryer before storing, to remove moisture. Down will mildew, so garments should be thoroughly dry before storage. If garment is rumpled and flat after storage, simply fluff in dryer at medium heat for an hour, to restore loft.

Down Sweater

Parts Identification: Sweater and lining parts are identical

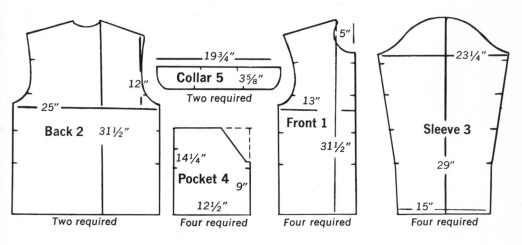

Back 2 31½"

25"

12"

Two required

Collar 5 3⅝"

19¾"

Two required

Pocket 4 9"

14¼"

12½"

Four required

Front 1

5"

13"

31½"

Four required

Sleeve 3

23¼"

29"

15"

Four required

All measurements are for size medium

Layout

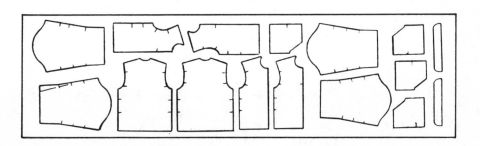

Down Sweater

3" Squares

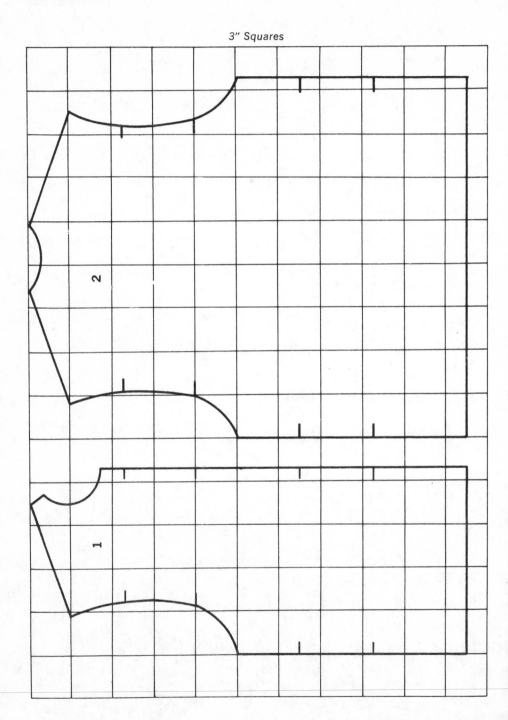

Down Sweater

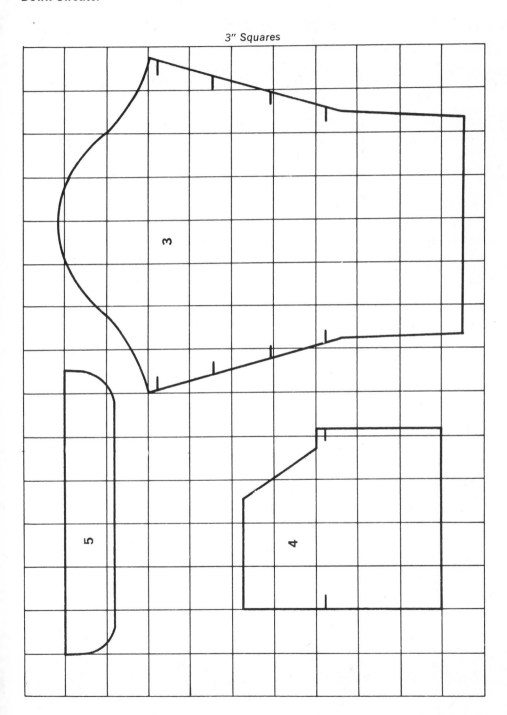

3" Squares

BIBLIOGRAPHY

Burton, Alan C., and Edholm, Otto G. *Man in a Cold Environment.* Williams and Wilkins Co., 1955. Reprint. New York: Hafner Press, 1970.

Crown, Fenya. *The Fabric Book for People Who Sew: Everything You Need to Know About the Fabrics You Buy.* New York: Grosset and Dunlap, 1973.

Cunningham, Gerry. *How to Enjoy Backpacking.* Boulder, Colorado: Colorado Outdoor Sports Corporation, 1969. Available at any Gerry dealer.

————. *How to Keep Warm.* Boulder, Colorado: Colorado Outdoor Sports Corporation, 1967. Available at any Gerry dealer.

Newburgh, L. H. *Physiology of Heat Regulation and the Science of Clothing.* W. B. Saunders Co., 1949. Reprint. New York: Hafner Press, 1968.

Quartermaster Research and Engineering, Environmental Protection Branch. *Physiology of Load Carrying.* Reports I–XIV, 1953–1957.

Quartermaster Research and Engineering. *A Proposed Method for Measuring the Filling Power of Down and Feathers.* Textile Series Report No. 48, 1951.

————. *Quartermaster Research on Water Resistant Textiles.* Textile Series Report No. 37, 1951.

Swirles, Frank M., Jr. *Basic Fabrics.* Frank M. Swirles, Jr., 1957.

Textile Research Journal. March 1955–current.

INDEX